Signing
FOR
DUMMIES®

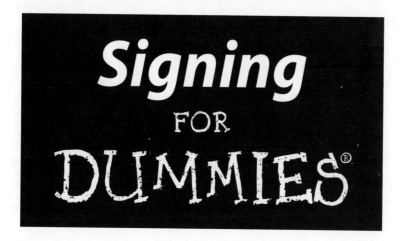

Signing
FOR
DUMMIES®

by Adan R. Penilla, II
and Angela Lee Taylor

WILEY

Wiley Publishing, Inc.

Signing For Dummies®

Published by
Wiley Publishing, Inc.
909 Third Avenue
New York, NY 10022
www.wiley.com

Copyright © 2003 by Wiley Publishing, Inc., Indianapolis, Indiana

Published simultaneously in Canada

About the Authors

Adan R. Penilla, II: Penilla is the President of the Colorado Registry of Interpreters: Pikes Peak Affiliate. He has his NAD IV interpreting certification and his legal qualification. In 1995, he was an interpreter at the World Federation of the Deaf in Vienna and is currently teaching ASL at Trinidad State Junior College. He has written an ASL Quick Study Bar Chart and WW II for the Deaf. He lectures on Sign language throughout the United States and is currently working on his PhD.

Angela Lee Taylor: Taylor, born deaf, is a native of Dixon, Illinois. Taylor graduated from Illinois School for the Deaf in 1985 and later received her bachelor's degree from Gallaudet University in 1997. During the past five years, Taylor has taught ASL for Pikes Peak Community College, Colorado School for the Deaf and the Blind, and the community. Taylor has annually coordinated for the statewide Deaf and Hard of Hearing Symposium for four years running. She is a tutor for the Shared Reading Project (SRP) and is also involved with ASLTAC. Taylor resides in Pueblo, Colorado with her husband, Lindsey, and border collie/blue heeler mix, Chip.

Dedication

(From lead author, Adan) To my parents, Adan and Aurora Penilla — mom and dad. Thanks for your generosity in love, patience, and giving. You have helped me more than you know.

Author's Acknowledgments

(From lead author, Adan) I would like to thank Mark Mattarocci. Real friends are hard to find, great friends even harder. Thank you for telling me what I needed to hear, not what I wanted to hear. Lindsey Antle, thanks for the knowledge of ASL you brought to this book; you gave me great confidence. A special thanks to Ron Hammer — your example in excellence is always before me, whether I like it or not. A deep thank you goes to my four sisters whose constant encouragement kept me going. Linda Barr, without your talent and genius this book would not have been published — thank you. Dr. Weaver and Dr. Cabbage, your support has helped a great deal. Thank you very much. Thanks to Sue Ann VonFeldt for her help during the research of this book.

Lastly, thank you Wiley Publishing, Inc. and crew for the opportunity to write for your company. I have learned much from you.

Publisher's Acknowledgments

We're proud of this book; please send us your comments through our Dummies online registration form located at www.dummies.com/register/.

Some of the people who helped bring this book to market include the following:

Acquisitions, Editorial, and Media Development

Project Editors: Jennifer Connolly, Kathleen Dobie

Acquisitions Editor: Natasha Graf

Copy Editor: Christina Guthrie

Technical Editor: Lindsey Antle, MA, RID Certified Interpreter (CSC, OIC:C)

Media Development Specialists: Megan Decraene, Angela Denny

Editorial Manager: Christine Meloy Beck

Editorial Assistants: Melissa Bennett, Elizabeth Rea

Cover Photos:
© Ghislain and Marie David de Lossey/ Getty Images/The Image Bank

Cartoons: Rich Tennant, www.the5thwave.com

Composition

Project Coordinator: Dale White

Layout and Graphics: Kelly Emkow, Shelley Norris, Rashell Smith, Julie Trippetti, Erin Zeltner

Special Art: Illustrator Lisa Reed

Proofreaders: Betty Kish, Charles Spencer

Indexer: Johnna VanHoose

Special Help
CD Producer: Her Voice Unlimited, LLC

CD Talent
CD Talent provided by Indiana School for the Deaf
Dave Tester, Teacher
Christine Wood, ASL Teacher
Donald Yates, Teacher Assistant
Diane Hazel Jones, ISD Outreach

Publishing and Editorial for Consumer Dummies

Diane Graves Steele, Vice President and Publisher, Consumer Dummies

Joyce Pepple, Acquisitions Director, Consumer Dummies

Kristin A. Cocks, Product Development Director, Consumer Dummies

Michael Spring, Vice President and Publisher, Travel

Brice Gosnell, Publishing Director, Travel

Suzanne Jannetta, Editorial Director, Travel

Publishing for Technology Dummies

Andy Cummings, Vice President and Publisher, Dummies Technology/General User

Composition Services

Gerry Fahey, Vice President of Production Services

Debbie Stailey, Director of Composition Services

Contents at a Glance

Table of Contents

Introduction

American Sign Language is something we've all seen Deaf people use in restaurants, hospitals, airports, and the like. It's fascinating to watch; to see people sharing ideas about every subject is remarkable. Now, you can have a chance to enter the wonderful world of Deaf people. This book is designed to act as an introduction for you to get your hands wet. It's also a great refresher for the person who needs an easy and clear way to practice Sign.

About This Book

Signing For Dummies is designed to give you a general understanding of the properties of Sign, as well as an understanding of Deaf culture. As you'll soon see, the language and the culture go hand in hand, and an understanding of both makes you a better signer.

To clarify, *Signing For Dummies* focuses solely on what's known as *American Sign Language* (ASL). ASL certainly isn't the only form of Sign Language that's used in the United States, but it is the most popular in the Deaf community, which is why we've chosen it over other Sign systems.

This book is categorized according to subject. You can use each chapter as a building block for the next chapter, or you can skip around wherever you please. Just find a subject that interests you and dig in, remembering that the most important thing is to have fun while you're figuring out this stuff. When you feel that you understand a concept, practice with your friends. If they understand you, you're probably on the right track. And if you don't understand something, don't despair. Talk to your Deaf friends or others who already know Sign.

Conventions Used in This Book

To help you navigate through this book, let us explain some conventions we've used when writing this book:

- ✔ **Glossing:** Whenever we use Sign in lists, examples, and dialogues, we print it in all caps to show that it's the closest equivalent to its English counterpart.

- ✔ **Bolding:** When we are about to introduce a new sign, we bold it in the text, so that you know you're about to learn a new Sign.

- ✔ **Capping of Sign and Deaf:** For the purposes of this book, we capitalize the word *Sign* as another name for the language and *Deaf* because it means culturally Deaf.

- ✔ **Dashes:** ASL doesn't use punctuation, so we add dashes to show slight pauses in Sign translations.

- ✔ The text (Sign and English translation) always comes before the illustration.

- ✔ To save space, words that are fingerspelled and manual numbers do not have illustrations. You can refer to Chapter 1 or the Cheat Sheet if you need help remembering how to sign a particular letter or number.

- ✔ "Sign" and "ASL" are used interchangeably.

- ✔ Web sites appear in `monofont`.

- ✔ Anytime you see a **Q** in a line of ASL, that indicates that you need to sign the manual question mark. Refer to Chapter 4 to find out more about the manual question mark.

This book also includes a few elements that other *For Dummies* books do not. Here are the new elements that you'll find:

- ✔ **Signin' the Sign dialogues:** Seeing Sign in actual context helps you understand how to use Sign vocabulary. Many signs have more than one meaning — this part can help out with that.

- ✔ **Fun & Games activities:** These visual games can help you practice Sign and are a good way to have fun while checking your progress.

The English sentences that are changed into American Sign Language (ASL) are not to be taken as word-for-word translations. In fact, many Signs have no English equivalents. Throughout this book, you find English equivalents that are close in meaning to Sign, but not exactly the same.

Foolish Assumptions

We hate to assume anything about anyone, but when writing this book, we had to make a few foolish assumptions about you. Here they are (we hope we were right):

- ✔ You have little or no experience in this type of communication, but you have a genuine interest.

✔ You don't expect to become fluent in Sign after going through this book. You just want some basic vocabulary, and you want to see what particular signs look like by themselves and in simple sentences.

✔ You aren't interested in memorizing grammar rules; you just want to communicate. (In case you do happen to be interested in ASL grammar, Chapter 2 is dedicated to that topic, and other rules and concepts are sprinkled throughout the book.)

✔ You want to know a few signs in order to be able to communicate with Deaf friends, family members, and acquaintances.

How This Book Is Organized

This book is divided by topic into parts, then further divided into chapters. The following sections let you know what kind of information you can find in each part.

Part 1: Signing On to Sign

This part lets you see by illustration and demonstration what fingerspelling looks and feels like. It explains how to use the basic hand shapes, facial expressions, and body language of Sign. Some rules are included, so that you can see how objects and action work together. You can make simple sentences with these basics.

Part 11: ASL in Action

In this part, you get to add vocabulary to your basic sentence structure. You also find ways to ask short questions, and after reading this section, you'll be able to practice your signing out and about the town.

Part 111: Signing On the Go

This part gives you Signs to help you get around easier. From giving and getting directions to different modes of transportation, you expand what you already know about Sign.

Part IV: Looking into Deaf Life

Come to this part for the Deaf perspective on life. Give your hands a rest and read how Deaf people function in a world that can hear.

Part V: The Part of Tens

Here you can find some great ideas to help you sign even better and faster. This part helps you get past any reluctance that you may feel and helps you feel more confident about signing in front of other people.

Part VI: Appendixes

This book has two appendixes. Appendix A gives you all the answers to the Fun & Games questions. Appendix B gives you detailed instructions for playing and using the CD that accompanies with this book.

Icons Used in This Book

To help you find certain types of information more easily, we've included several icons in this book. You find them on the left-hand side of the page, sprinkled throughout:

This icon highlights tips and tricks that can make signing easier.

This icon points out interesting and important information that you don't want to forget.

To avoid making a blunder or offending a Deaf friend, pay attention to what these paragraphs have to say.

For those grammar buffs out there, this icon points out useful ASL grammar rules and concepts.

This icon draws your attention to pieces of information about the culture of the Deaf community.

This icon highlights text that you also find on the CD. Many Signin' the Sign dialogues appear on the CD, so you can practice with the Signers.

Where to Go from Here

The beauty of this book is that you can go anywhere you want. You may find it helpful to start with the first two chapters to get down the basics, but if that's not your thing, feel free to jump in wherever you want. Find a subject that interests you, start signing, and have fun!

Part I
Signing On to Sign

The 5th Wave   By Rich Tennant

"Okay, don't get agitated if you can't remember the Sign for something. Just spell it out real slow and easy."

In this part . . .

These chapters use what you already know about Sign and give you a little bit more. This part introduces you to fingerspelling, sending a message by using facial expressions, and putting together simple sentences in Sign.

Chapter 1

Finding Out That You Already Know a Little Sign

In This Chapter

▶ Expressing Signs that look like what they mean

▶ Discovering the Signing basics

Signing isn't difficult, although moving your hands, body, and face to convey meaning instead of just your voice may seem odd at first. Your reward, however, is being able to meet and communicate with a whole new group of people. That's definitely worth the initial awkwardness!

This chapter illustrates the manual alphabet and talks some about numbers. Here, we show you the basics of making handshapes and using your facial expression and body language to get your ideas across. And, we start off by reassuring you that you already know some Signs. Trust us — you do.

Discovering Signs That Look Like What They Mean

Iconic or *natural Signs* look like what they mean — the up and down motion of brushing your teeth that means **toothbrush,** the right and left punches that mean **boxing.** Here are some examples:

BOXING: Looks like you're "putting up your dukes."

DRIVE: Pretend that you're steering a car.

EAT: Act like you're putting food in your mouth.

MILK: Have you ever seen a cow being milked? That's how you sign milk.

SWIMMING/POOL: Think of when you walk through the shallow end of the pool and extend your arms out in front of you to clear the water.

TOOTHBRUSH/BRUSH TEETH: If you've ever brushed your teeth with your finger, you made the Sign for toothbrush and for brushing your teeth.

Like the Sign for boxing, many sports Signs are iconic. Check out Chapter 8 for more sports Signs.

Building on the Basics of Sign — Gestures and Expression

You already know that "speaking" American Sign Language (ASL) is mostly a matter of using your fingers, hands, and arms. What you may not understand yet is that your facial expression and body language are important and sometimes crucial for understanding Signs and their meaning.

The following sections explain how you get nearly your whole body involved in ASL.

Spelling with your fingers

Signers use the manual alphabet all the time, especially beginners. People's names, at first, and some words need to be *fingerspelled* — spelling words using the manual alphabet. So, as a beginner, feel free to fingerspell any word you don't know the Sign for. If you want to fingerspell two or more words in a row such as a title or first and last name of someone, pause for just a second between each word.

In this book, a word that you fingerspell is shown in hyphenated letters. For example: *Mall* is written as M-A-L-L. We usually don't take the space to show the hand Signs for each letter; we leave it to you to find the appropriate letters here in this chapter as well as on the Cheat Sheet at the front of this book.

Don't worry about being slow at fingerspelling. Remember, clarity is the goal, not speed. Silently mouth the letters as you fingerspell them. Doing so helps you to control your speed because you're concentrating more on the letters.

Being a winning receiver

If you have trouble reading someone's Signs, look to the context and ask yourself, "What could this person mean?" And remember that it's okay to ask someone to repeat something, just like you do when you don't understand someone speaking to you. You can show a Signer you're "listening" by nodding your head. Watch the whole person — the eyes, face, hands, and body movements tell the whole story.

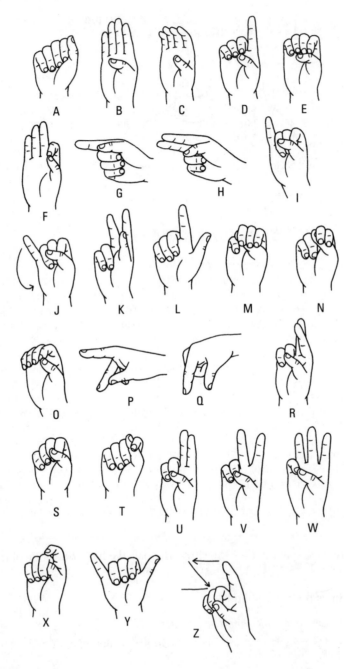

Some *initializations* — concepts such as **a.m.** and **p.m.** — are signed as morning and evening, respectively, rather than fingerspelled. But a word like **okay** can be fingerspelled as O-K, or you can just show the F handshape.

A.M.

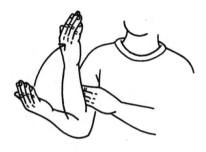

P.M.

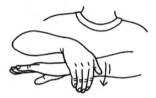

Shaping up those hands

Remembering a few simple points can help you make *handshapes* like a lifelong Signer. Handshapes are hand formations used to sign each letter of the alphabet. In this section, we explain the basic conventions.

For Signing purposes, the hand you write with is called your *dominant hand* (some folks call it the *active hand*). The other hand is your *base hand* or *passive hand*. In this book, all of the illustrations represent a right-handed Signer. So the right hand illustrates the dominant hand, and the left hand illustrates the passive hand.

While the active hand does the work, the passive hand does one of the following:

✔ Mimics the active hand

✔ Mirrors the active hand

✔ Displays one of seven basic handshapes, called *natural handshapes*

The seven natural handshapes are the letters **A, B, C, S,** and **O** as well as the numbers **1** and **5.**

Natural handshapes can be used in a variety of ways — the same handshape may move for a particular Sign but not another, or the same handshape may be formed in one direction for a particular Sign but formed in a different direction for another. For one Sign, such as **start,** the natural handshape (in this case, the number 5) forms in one direction. But in another Sign, such as **cook,** that same natural handshape is formed in a different direction. Check out the following examples of active/passive handshapes used while signing:

 START: Place your active index finger between your index and middle fingers of your passive hand, and then turn the active index finger outward — it looks like you're turning the ignition key in a car.

 BUY: Hold out your passive hand, palm up in the 5 hand-shape. Use your active hand as you would to hand money to a salesclerk.

 COOK: Hold your passive hand out, palm up. Lay your active hand across the top of it, palm down. Now flip your active hand over, palm up, then flip it back over, palm down.

When the passive hand mimics or mirrors the shape of the dominant hand, both hands either move together or alternately. If moving alternately, you move both hands in alternate directions at the same time. Examples of alternating handshapes include:

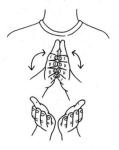

BOOK: Make this Sign as if you're actually opening a book.

GIFT: Both hands in front of you in the "X" handshape, but one is extended a little farther away than the other from your body. At the same time, jerk your hands up a little bit, twice.

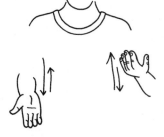

MAYBE

STORE: Keep your hands in the same shape and move them back and forth simultaneously.

Benefiting with body language

Communicating a concept in Sign is often made clear by using body language. The meaning of **"I don't know"** comes through clearly when you raise your shoulders, tilt your head, and turn your palm up. Signing **"I'm sick"** is more easily understood when you accompany the Sign with half-shut eyes, open mouth, and a partially extended tongue. Another example is the word **no.** The speed at which you shake your head from side to side, with eyes open or shut, can say a lot about the degree of **"no."** Check out the illustrations of these Signs to see what we mean.

DON'T KNOW

SICK: Both hands move in a small circular motion.

NO: When you sign the word, close your eyes if you want to make it more emphatic.

Telling with your face

In Sign, you use your face to show emotion and add expression. Facial expression tells you what type of sentence is being signed and how the Signer feels about the information. Your facial expression is just as important as what your hands are doing. Sign these expressions as if you actually "feel" that way. For example, you sign the word **sad** while you slump your shoulders down and make a sad facial expression. You sign **happy** just the opposite — keep your shoulders up and wear a smile. (Check out Chapter 3 for illustrations of these Signs.)

Be sure that you maintain eye contact when you're signing, and watch your conversational partner's face, not his or her hands. Your peripheral vision allows you to still see the hands, so don't worry about missing any Signs.

Signin' the Sign

Belinda and Terry are getting ready for the holidays. Belinda wants to start shopping for Christmas presents.

Terry: Do you want a ride to the mall?
Sign: M-A-L-L — RIDE — WANT YOU Q

 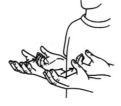 

Belinda: Yes, I want to start buying Christmas gifts soon.
Sign: YES — SOON — CHRISTMAS GIFTS — START
BUYING — WANT ME

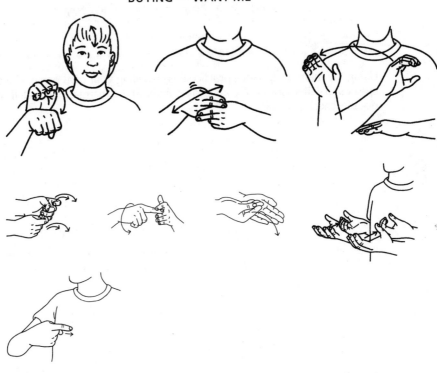

Fun and Games

● ●

Using the manual alphabet, practice fingerspelling your own name. Then finger-spell ten 3-letter words of your choice. Refer to the manual alphabet, if needed, to double-check yourself.

● ●

Chapter 2

Digging into Grammar and Numbers

*I*n this chapter, we talk about the building blocks that you need to communicate in any language — nouns, verbs, adjectives, and adverbs — and we tell you how to put them together to form simple sentences. We also tell you how to get your body involved to express verb tenses.

Numbers are also pretty basic to understanding any language, so we talk about them in this chapter on basics, too.

Explaining the Parts of Speech

Both English and ASL have subjects and verbs, as well as adjectives and adverbs that describe the subjects and verbs. Also, English and Sign both allow you to converse about the present, past, and future, so whatever English can do, Sign can do — visually. However, unlike English, ASL does not use prepositions as a separate part of speech. As a general rule, most prepositions in Sign, with a few exceptions, act as verbs.

The English language articles — *a, an,* and *the* — are not used in Sign. Likewise, helping verbs, such as *am, is,* and *are,* aren't used in Sign, either. Passive languages, such as English, use helping verbs. Sign is an active language in which helping (passive) verbs aren't necessary.

Distinguishing between noun/verb pairs

Some nouns and verbs in Sign share the same handshapes. You distinguish the part of speech by signing the motion once if it's a verb and twice if it's a noun.

Though most nouns don't have a verb that looks the same, all but a few nouns need the double motion. Most of the noun illustrations in this book are represented by double arrows. We let you know about nouns that don't follow the double-motion rule.

Table 2-1 shows a few noun and verb pairs.

Table 2-1		Nouns and Verbs with Shared Handshapes	
English Noun	*Sign*	*English Verb*	*Sign*
CHAIR		SIT	
PLANE		FLY	
CAR		DRIVE	

The following examples compare the noun/verb differences.

English: Please sit in this chair.
Sign: THIS CHAIR (point) — PLEASE — SIT

English: I like to fly small planes.
Sign: SMALL PLANES — FLY — LIKE ME

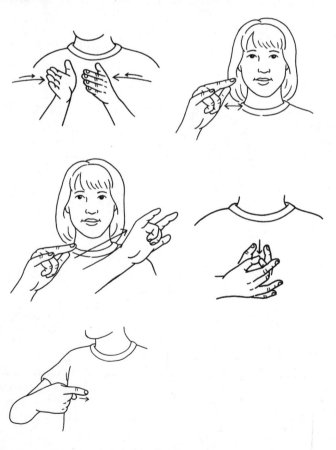

Modifying with adjectives and adverbs

In English, a modifier can come before or after the word it's modifying, depending on the sentence. However, in Sign, you typically place the adjective or adverb — the modifier — after the word that it modifies, although, sometimes in Sign, you may find yourself expressing the modifier at the same time you sign the word it modifies — just by using your face.

Your facial expressions can describe things and actions in ASL. For instance, if something is small or big, you can show the extent of it as you sign without actually signing "small" or "big." Instead, use facial expressions. For example, you can describe a small piece of thread by pursing your lips, blowing out a little air and closing your eyes halfway. If something is very thick, puff out your cheeks. You can convey that it's raining hard or that a car is moving fast by moving your eyebrows or shaping your mouth a certain way. (Turn to Chapter 1 for a discussion about using expressions and body language.)

The following examples give you a good idea of some of the different facial expressions you may use to get your point across when describing things in Sign:

PRETTY GIRL: Raise your eyebrows, form your mouth into an "o" shape (like saying ooh), sign "pretty" and then "girl."

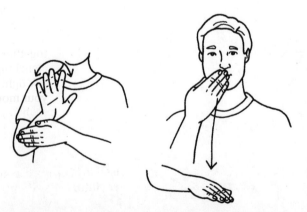

BAD MOVIE: Sign the word "movie" and then turn your mouth down in a frown and scrunch your eyebrows together while signing the word "bad."

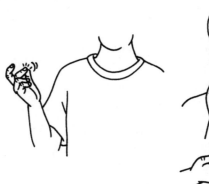

GOOD DOG: Sign the word "dog" first, then slightly smile and raise your eyebrows as you sign the word "good."

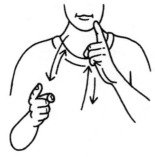

TALK LOUDLY or **LOUDLY TALK**

RUN VERY FAST: Sign the word "run" while scrunching your eyebrows together and clenching your jaw tight with your mouth slightly open.

Some adverbs used in English are not usually used in Sign, such as the words "very" and "really." You have to incorporate them into the verb by using facial expressions.

Talking Tenses

To communicate tenses in Sign, you need your hands *and* your body. Think of your body as being in the present tense — it's a fairly safe assumption, we hope.

Showing tense in ASL is partly a matter of where you sign in relation to your body.

Signing in **present tense** is pretty simple — you sign close to your body, just like you normally do in a signed conversation. That's all there is to it!

Signing in **past tense** is just a bit trickier. To place everything you sign into past tense, you sign **finish** at chest level either at the beginning or end of the sentence while saying the word "fish," a shortened version of "finish." This signals that everything has already happened. Although it doesn't matter whether you sign the word finish at the beginning or end of the sentence, most Signers place it at the beginning.

You can also use the finish sign when making an exclamation. (For more on this Sign's uses, see the section titled, "Exclaiming in Simple Sentences," later in this chapter.)

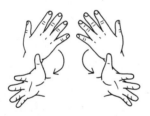

Participles ("to" plus a verb) and **perfect tenses** (should have been, etc.) are technically passive tenses, which are not used in ASL, as explained in "Explaining the Parts of Speech" earlier in this chapter.

Signing in **future tense** works pretty much the same way as signing in past tense. You indicate future tense by signing and saying **will** at the end of a sentence. The farther you sign the word will from the front of your body, the farther into the future you go. Here's an example:

English: He can go later.
Sign: HE GO — WILL

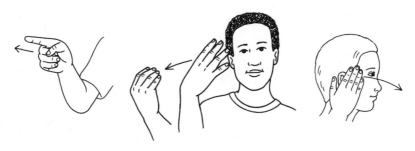

You can also sign **will** to show affirmation. For example:

English: Mike is walking over to my house.
Sign: MY HOUSE — M-I-K-E — WALKING — WILL

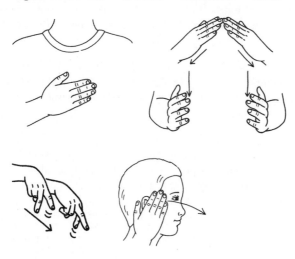

You can easily sign an event that is going to happen in the future. A simple rule to follow: Mention what is planned or intended, then sign "will."

Here's a time-sensitive concept that doesn't quite fit into past, present, or future. To show that you're not yet finished or that you haven't even started a task, sign the unaccomplished deed, then sign **not yet** while shaking your head slightly from side to side, as if saying "no," at the end of the sentence. You don't pronounce "not yet," though; you simply sign it. The following sentence gives you an idea of how you can use this expression:

English: I haven't eaten.
Sign: ME EAT — NOT YET

Structuring Sentences

Putting a sentence together in English is pretty basic. You usually put it in subject-verb-direct object order, perhaps throwing in an indirect object between the verb and the direct object. In ASL, however, you can choose to assemble your sentence in different orders, depending on the content of your dialogue.

Some sentences should only be signed in a natural English order because rearranging them would cause confusion. However, most of the time, you can get your point across in a variety of ways without worrying about the word order.

Sign is not a written language. It is a form of communication passed down through generations of the Deaf. Some people have attempted to make an artificial sign system for writing purposes, but few people know it because its use is so limited. Consequently, ASL has no punctuation because, in its natural state, it isn't meant to be a written language. To write about Sign, as in this book, you must translate it as closely as possible into a written language such as English.

Subjecting yourself to nouns and verbs in simple sentences

Unlike English grammar rules, which dictate that the subject must go before the verb, Sign allows you to put the subject before or after the verb when dealing with simple sentences; it doesn't matter which word comes first. The same goes for exclamations; you can place them either at the beginning or the end of a simple sentence. See the section "Exclaiming in Simple Sentences" later in this chapter. The following examples illustrate how simple sentences work.

English: He ran.
Sign: HE RAN
Sign: RAN HIM

English: She fell.
Sign: SHE FELL
Sign: FELL HER

Placing subjects and objects

Start with a basic subject-verb sentence. You can sign it either in subject-verb or verb-subject order. Here are some examples:

English: He sells.
Sign: HE SELLS

English: I eat.
Sign: ME EAT

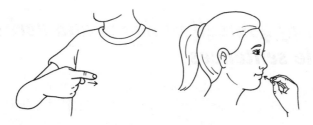

English: She drives.
Sign: SHE DRIVES

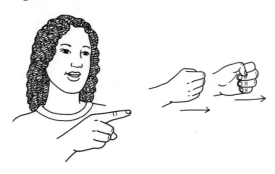

Although these tiny sentences get the point across, the world would be pretty boring if that's how people communicated all the time. So add a direct object to each of these sentences to make them a little more interesting.

In case you haven't had a grammar class in a few years, a *direct object* is a word that goes after the verb and answers the question "What?" or "Whom?" However, in ASL, the direct object can go either before the subject or after the verb.

English: He sells food.
Sign: HE SELLS FOOD

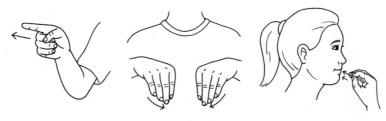

Sign: FOOD HE SELLS

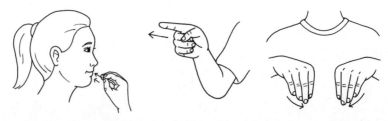

English: I eat pizza.
Sign: ME EAT PIZZA

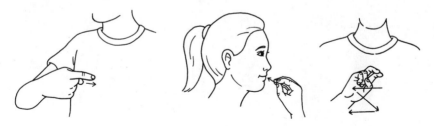

Sign: PIZZA ME EAT

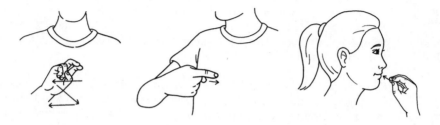

English: She drives a car.
Sign: SHE DRIVES CAR

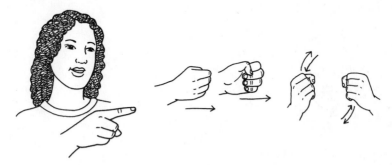

Sign: CAR SHE DRIVES

 If you have a sentence that may be misunderstood if you change the word order, leave it in the natural English order. For example, if you want to say "Joe loves Sue," you need to sign JOE LOVES SUE. Changing it around to SUE LOVES JOE doesn't convey the same meaning. (Having said that, we really hope that Sue does love Joe in return.)

Okay. So you're signing sentences with direct objects. Now, try to take your Signing skills one step further by signing *indirect objects*. (Another quick grammar reminder: Indirect objects are words that come between the verb and direct object; they indicate who or what receives the direct object.) You place the indirect object right after the subject and then show the action. These sentences show you the correct order.

English: The girl throws the dog a bone.
Sign: GIRL — DOG BONE — THROW

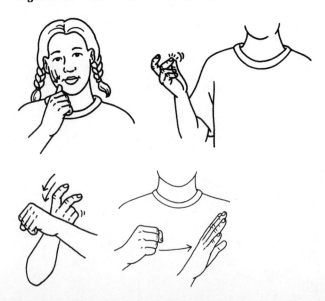

English: I give the teacher apples.
Sign: ME TEACHER — APPLES GIVE

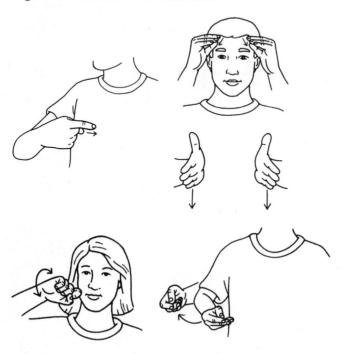

 Signing sentences in an understandable order may be a bit tricky at first. If the person you're signing to is leaning forward, has an inquisitive look, or seems distracted, he or she probably doesn't understand you. You may want to try signing that sentence again.

Signin' the Sign

 Linda and Buddy are at work. The restaurant will be opening in one hour, and they're taking a quick breather before it opens.

Linda: The chairs look nice.
Sign: CHAIRS — LOOK NICE

Buddy: That pizza smells good.
Sign: PIZZA — SMELLS GOOD

Linda: We're finished. I'm going to eat now.
Sign: WE FINISH — NOW — ME EAT

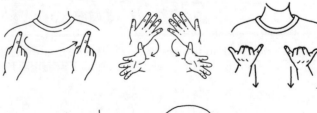

Buddy: Sit. I'll bring you some pizza.
Sign: SIT — PIZZA — BRING YOU WILL

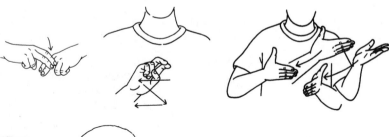

Linda: Throw me an apple, too.
Sign: APPLE THROW ME TOO

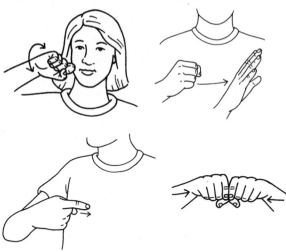

Exclaiming in Simple Sentences

Exclamations in all languages tell the listener how you feel about a subject. Sign is no different. Exclamation is used a lot in Sign; both Signer and receiver use it. As in English, you can also use exclamation to show *how* strong you feel or don't feel about something. Other signers who are watching can sign what they feel about what you've signed, too. Exclamations can be signed at the beginning or end of the sentence. Most, but not all, exclamations in Sign have English equivalents. Following is a list of some of the more popular Sign exclamations:

OH/I SEE

WHAT: This exclamation is fingerspelled simply as W-T; it's only used as a one-word exclamation (as in "What?!")

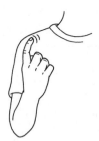

COME ON

FINISH: Although finish is used at the beginning of a sentence to show past tense (see the section, "Talking Tenses," earlier in this chapter), it's also used as humor in Sign to indicate "enough already" and as a reprimand meaning "stop that." You sign the word, using just one hand, and you pronounce the word "fish," which is a shortened version of the Sign for "finish," as stated earlier. You can tell by the context of the conversation as to which way it's being used.

OH MY GOSH

WOW

OOH: (Also known as a "flick"): Start with your hand in the "8" sign handshape, then change it to a "5" sign handshape, using a quick flicking motion with your middle finger.

COOL

Signin' the Sign

 Adan and Aurora will be celebrating their fiftieth wedding anniversary. Adan wants to stay home and celebrate, while Aurora wants to go out. See how their conversation unfolds.

Aurora: Wow! Our fiftieth anniversary!
Sign: ANNIVERSARY — FIFTY YEARS — US — WOW

Adan: Ooh, that's a long time!
Sign: (flick!) — LONG TIME — SO FAR

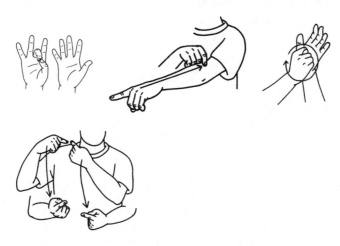

Aurora: Where do you want to celebrate?
Sign: CELEBRATION — WHERE GO — Q

Adan: The living room.
Sign: (point) — LIVING ROOM

Aurora: Oh, I see. Why?
Sign: OH I SEE WHY — Q

Adan: It's inexpensive.
Sign: CHEAP

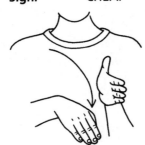

Aurora: You stop that!
Sign: FINISH

Counting on Numbers

Did you know that counting in Sign can be done in 27 different ways? That's a pretty cool piece of trivia, but for this book, we just concentrate on two of those ways — using cardinal and ordinal numbers. If you'd like to check out some other ways to count, Gallaudet University and the National Technical Institute of the Deaf are great resources.

Cardinal (counting) and ordinal (ordering) numbers will get you through everyday situations, such as counting the millions you won on the lottery, giving your address and phone number to the movie star who wants to get to know you better, telling your mom that you won the first Pulitzer prize for hip-hop poetry, and telling Cinderella that it's midnight.

When you want to specify that there's more than one item — plural — you sign the item first, followed by the quantity. Unlike English, you don't have to change the item to a plural by adding "s." A good way to remember this is to keep in mind that you need to show what the item is before you can tell someone how many. For example:

English: two books
Sign: BOOK TWO

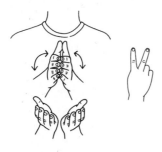

English: four cars
Sign: CAR FOUR

Getting from one to ten with cardinal numbers

Being able to give numerical information in ASL opens many doors. You can give someone your phone number, make an appointment, and warn a potential guest that you have 12, yes 12, cats.

When you're indicating quantity and counting things, sign the numbers 1 through 5 and 11 through 15 with your palm facing you, and the numbers 6 through 10 and 16 through 19 with your palm facing the person to whom you're signing.

Just as in English, there are exceptions to every rule, especially the one about which way your palm faces. To tell time in Sign, let your dominant (active) index finger touch your other wrist — where you would wear a watch. Then use your dominant hand to sign the appropriate hour (number) with your palm facing the person you're signing to; the same goes for addresses and phone numbers. For quantity, though, the numbers 1 through 5 have your palm facing you; 6 through 10 have your palm facing the addressee.

Table 2-2 gives you numbers 1 through 19.

Table 2-2		Cardinal Numbers	
English	*Sign*	*English*	*Sign*
ONE		TWO	
THREE		FOUR	
FIVE		SIX	
SEVEN		EIGHT	

English	Sign	English	Sign
NINE		TEN	
ELEVEN		TWELVE	
THIRTEEN		FOURTEEN	
FIFTEEN		SIXTEEN	
SEVENTEEN		EIGHTEEN	
NINETEEN			

To sign decade numbers — 30, 40, 50, and so on — you sign the first number (3, 4, 5) followed by the Sign for the number 0. You sign "hundreds," such as 600, 700, 800, and so on, by first signing the number (6, 7, 8), then the Sign for "hundred," as the following examples show:

THIRTY (30)

FORTY (40)

FIFTY (50)

SIX HUNDRED
(600)

SEVEN HUNDRED
(700)

EIGHT HUNDRED
(800)

Ordering ordinal numbers

Ordinal numbers show orderly placement: first cup of coffee, second chapter, and third base, for example. To indicate an ordinal number in ASL, twist your wrist inward while signing the respective number.

FIRST

SECOND

THIRD

Signin' the Sign

 Ted is going to Della's house for a visit. Della is giving Ted directions in hopes that he will arrive on time.

Della: Can you come over to my house at 7:00?
Sign: 7:00 P.M. — MY HOUSE — COME — CAN YOU — Q

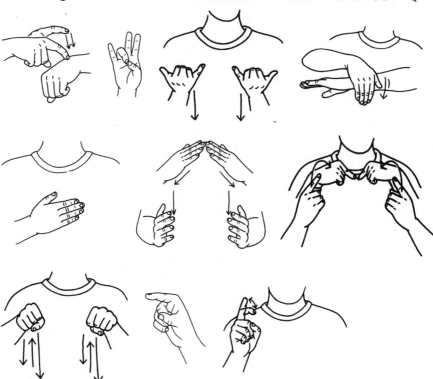

Ted: Yes, I can.
Sign: YES — CAN ME

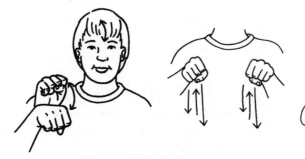

Della: Remember, it's 329 West Drive.
Sign: REMEMBER — HOUSE — WEST — D-R — 3-2-9

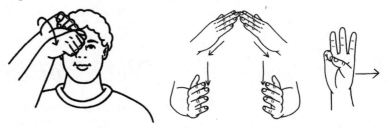

Ted: Can you give me directions?
Sign: DIRECTIONS — ME — CAN YOU — Q

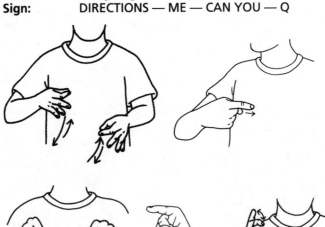

Ted:	Right on West Drive; the third house on the right.
Sign:	HOUSE — THIRD RIGHT — STREET — WEST - D-R

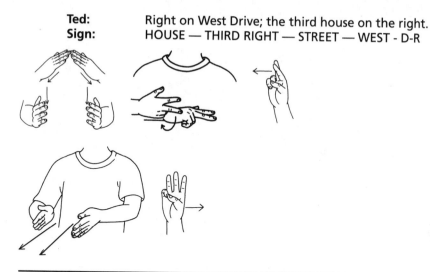

Personification: The Secret of Agents

In ASL, turning a verb into a person is called *personification*. You do it with two simple motions: Sign the verb and then glide the heels of your hands down the sides of your body with your fingers extended outward. The result of this is an **agent.** Look at this next list to see what we mean.

WRITE + AGENT = WRITER

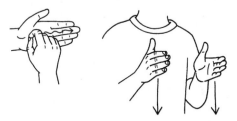

FLY + AGENT = PILOT

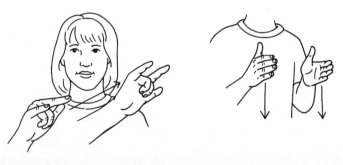

SUPERVISE + AGENT = SUPERVISOR

COOK + AGENT = CHEF

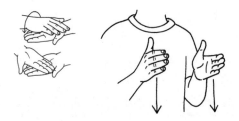

LAW + AGENT = LAWYER

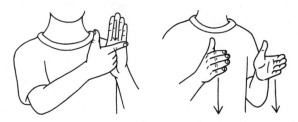

MANAGE + AGENT = MANAGER

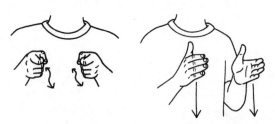

Fun & Games

Using the following pictures, recall what each Sign means, then fill in the blanks. If you need help, the answers are in Appendix A.

a.

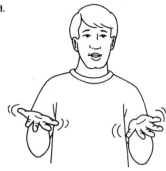

b.

c.

d.

e.

f.

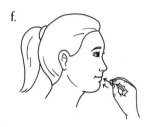

g.

h.

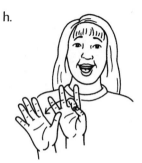

(continued)

1. My picture won _____ place.

2. _____ that's interesting!

3. Our plane leaves at _____.

4. I _____ pizza at the mall.

5. We live on a _____ farm, with hundreds of acres of crops.

6. The _____ is broken, so I'm afraid to _____ on it.

7. I don't like to _____ in small _____; being inside clouds scares me.

8. _____?! That doesn't make any sense.

• •

Part II
ASL in Action

The 5th Wave   By Rich Tennant

GUNTHER INVENTED HIS OWN UNIQUE WAY OF ADDING AN EXCLAMATION POINT TO HIS SIGNING.

In this part . . .

These chapters get you going in basic conversation. You get a taste of the following: starting conversations, meeting people, going out, enjoying hobbies and sports, talking shop, and touring your home and office. After reading these chapters, you'll be ready for a night on the town with Deaf friends.

Chapter 3

Introductions and Greetings

. . . .

In This Chapter

▶ Getting someone's attention

▶ Expressing how you feel

▶ Signing other countries

▶ Describing scenery

. . . .

*T*his chapter sets you off on the right foot (or hand!) to meet and greet fellow Signers by giving you tips on how to start a conversation with Deaf people. Telling Signers how you feel about the world around you is a great conversation starter. Describing where you live and where you would like to go will keep your conversation going until your hands fall off. You can acquaint yourself with ASL by watching Deaf people sign. Being included in a conversation is a great transition for conversing in ASL. Don't worry about signing perfectly. Deaf people will know that you're a novice Signer — just have fun with it.

Your initiation and a question about ASL, sports, or any popular restaurant can also start a conversation. This chapter gives you some great ideas on expressing yourself as you get acquainted with Deaf people.

Keep in mind that when someone asks you your name, sign your first and last name — it's good manners.

Interacting with other Signers is an important part of getting the basics under your belt. You'll find that all Signers, Deaf and hearing, have different styles; no two people sign the same. Like English, words are the same, but no two people talk alike. Setting a goal to be clear is a must. Your style will come naturally.

Getting the Conversational Ball Rolling

Most people who learn Sign look forward to signing with others. Attending functions with other Signers gives ample opportunity to practice Sign. At

Deaf functions, signed conversation happens everywhere. If you're invited by a Deaf person, allow him or her to introduce you to the others — great conversations start this way. If Deaf people correct your Signing, view this as a compliment and take no offense. They see you as a worthy investment.

Getting someone's attention

Attracting someone's attention is easy in English. A simple yell turns many heads. To get a Deaf person's attention, tap him or her on the shoulder or the back of the arm between the elbow and the shoulder. Waving at someone is another good way. Having wooden floors is also a big help — stomping on the floor is an acceptable and popular attention-getter. Deaf people feel the vibration on the floor and turn to see its origination.

Another way to get someone's attention is to make and maintain eye contact. You can tell someone across a crowded room that you have something on your mind by catching his or her eye. And then, after eye contact has been made and you've approached one another, you can proceed with a conversation. Non-signers may view this action as staring and think that it's rude, but in the world of Sign, making and maintaining eye contact is a necessary common practice.

Never throw objects at a Deaf person to get his or her attention. Besides being just plain rude, it's also dangerous. ASL is a visual language, so Deaf people really value their eyesight. Accidentally hitting someone in the eye could be devastating, and you could get hit back!

Conversation starters

Asking questions is probably the most popular way to start a conversation. You can ask a person's name, sign yours, ask what school a person attended, and so on. Many Deaf people attended one of the residential schools for the Deaf that are located throughout the United States; you may have a city in common. You can also start a conversation with a simple **hi** or **hello,** followed by **nice to meet you.** These greetings work with Deaf people of all ages. Signing **What's up?** is a simple, informal greeting that's a great opener, too.

Shaking hands and giving hugs are also common additions to Deaf greetings. Hand shaking is more formal than hugging, just as is true in the hearing world.

You can join a conversation easily by using one of the following openings:

HI/HELLO

GOODBYE

NICE TO MEET YOU

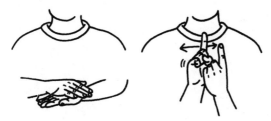

Raised eyebrows and head tilted forward show others that your sentence is a question and that you're waiting for a response. Try these simple questions:

English: Do you sign?
Sign: SIGN YOU Q

English: Are you deaf?
Sign: DEAF YOU Q

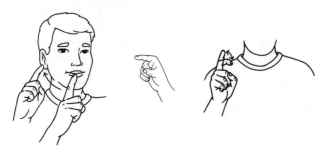

English: How are you?
Sign: WHAT'S UP

Don't pretend to be Deaf just to be able to practice your signing skills. In the Deaf community, as everywhere else, deception leads to mistrust, and promoting mistrust is a bad idea.

When you see two people standing close together and signing small, don't stare. They may be having a private conversation.

Chewing gum is a no-no in Sign. Mouth movement is an important part of Signed communications. Do everyone a favor and keep chewing and signing separate.

Signin' the Sign

Buddy and Della are at the park. Buddy sees Della make a gesture that looks like a Sign and decides to approach her.

Buddy: Do you sign?
Sign: SIGN YOU Q

Della: Yes, are you deaf?
Sign: YES — DEAF YOU Q

Buddy: No, my sister is deaf.
Sign: NO — MY SISTER — DEAF

 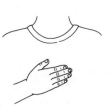  

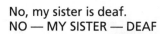

Della: Oh, I see; you sign well.
Sign: OH I SEE — SIGN SKILL YOU

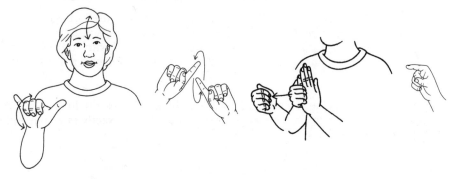

Getting Acquainted

TIP

As you get acquainted with folks, keep these tips in mind:

- **During introductions, simply *fingerspell* (sign each letter individually) your name.** Deaf people are the only ones who give *name Signs*. Those who can hear, the hearing, don't invent their own, nor do they give name Signs to each other. (See the nearby sidebar for more on what exactly name Signs are.)

- **Follow the conversation that's started — understand what you can.** If you don't catch something, don't interrupt the Signer. Wait until she's finished.

- **Keep a steady hand.** Your Signs are easier to read when your hand isn't shaking.

- **Ask questions for clarification.** Don't be embarrassed if you didn't understand something. Asking questions is the best way to learn.

What's in a name Sign?

Name Signs aren't formal names; they're manual letters that express some characteristic of a person or even just a manual letter or letters that represent someone's name. Name Signs are manual handshapes that you use to signify a person. Having a name Sign allows everyone in the Deaf community to know who you're talking about and helps avoid constantly having to fingerspell someone's name. Name Signs are signed on the Signer's body or in front of the Signer. You normally make the handshape of the first letter of a person's first name and, sometimes, last name(s).

Addressing people

When introducing yourself to others in Sign, you use both first and last names. Sign doesn't use titles that are used in English, such as Mr., Mrs., ma'am, or sir. If a Signer who's Deaf will have continual contact with someone, that person's name will be fingerspelled, or the Deaf person will give a name Sign to him or her.

Pointing, like staring, isn't polite in the hearing world. In Sign, however, pointing is appropriate because it lets people know exactly to whom and what you're referring.

Talking about where you're from

Signing about where you're from is a great way to converse with a new friend. Because it can lead to other topics of conversation, it's a common ice-breaker and will help you practice your Sign vocabulary. You can practice your fingerspelling — you may not know the Sign of a particular location, or it may not have a Sign — and expand your geographical knowledge. For example, you could sign about different famous landmarks and tourist sites.

Signin' the Sign

Cameron and Della are meeting Dee and Ted for the first time. They're making their introductions.

Dee: Hi, I'm Dee.
Sign: HI — D-E-E ME

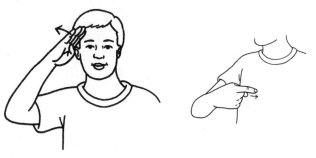

Ted: I'm Dee's husband, Ted.
Sign: ME T-E-D — D-E-E HUSBAND

Cameron: Nice to meet you. I'm Cameron.
Sign: NICE MEET YOU (plural) — C-A-M-E-R-O-N ME

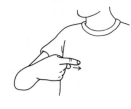

Della: And I'm Della. Nice to meet you, too.
Sign: ME D-E-L-L-A — NICE MEET TOO

Sharing feelings and emotions

Sharing your feelings and emotions when signing is easy because Sign is naturally so expressive. Put your heart into what you're signing to genuinely express what you mean. Some feelings and emotions can be transmitted with minimal Sign and a lot of facial expression because people can already understand them easily.

Take a look at some Signs for feelings and emotions:

SAD

HAPPY

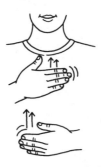

ANGRY

Signin' the Sign

Dee and Buddy are at the store. Dee is shocked by the rising cost of everything. She shares her displeasure with Buddy.

Dee: Everything is so expensive!
Sign: EVERYTHING EXPENSIVE

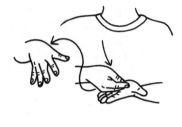

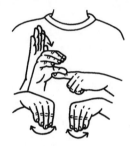

Buddy: Yes, and no sales.
Sign: TRUE — DISCOUNTS NONE

Dee: It's sad; even stamps are going up.
Sign: SAD — STAMP COST — INCREASE TOO

Buddy: It really makes me angry.
Sign: ANGRY ME

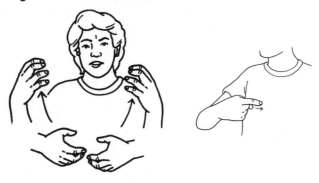

Dee: Me, too.
Sign: ME TOO

Talking countries

Signing in every country is different. Although some countries have similar Sign languages, no two are exactly alike.

When two Deaf people from different countries meet, their chances of communicating are pretty good because they're both skilled at making their points known in their respective countries. Although their Sign languages are different, their communication skills may involve mime, writing, gestures, and pointing. People who can hear can also do those things, but their communication skills are usually more dependent on the spoken languages.

Some country name Signs that are used in ASL are offensive to those respective countries. For instance, the ASL Sign for Mexico also means "bandit," and the Signs for Korea, Japan, and China are signed near the eye with a hand movement that indicates "slanted eyes." Many Signers are now using the indigenous name Signs that are politically correct and aren't offensive.

Here are the Signs for the countries in North America:

CANADA

U.S. (United States)/AMERICA

MEXICO

Here are the Signs for some European countries:

ENGLAND

FRANCE

SPAIN

Signin' the Sign

Paula and Ken are going to Europe. They're visiting several countries and are discussing their itinerary.

Ken: Great! We're going to Europe!
Sign: GREAT — EUROPE — YOU ME GO

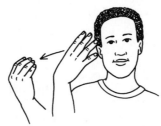

Paula: I'm so excited about seeing Italy.
Sign: EXCITED ME — ITALY SEE

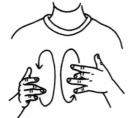

Paula: The sunsets are beautiful in Milan.
Sign: M-I-L-A-N SUNSETS BEAUTIFUL

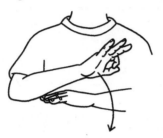

Naming states and cities

Many states and cities have name Signs or abbreviations, but it's okay to ask someone to fingerspell a place if you don't understand.

Some common state and city Signs are in Table 3-1.

Table 3-1	Signs for Various Cities and States		
English	*Sign*	*English*	*Sign*
ARIZONA		ATLANTA	
CALIFORNIA		BOSTON	

English	Sign	English	Sign
COLORADO		DALLAS	
FLORIDA		DENVER	
KENTUCKY		HOUSTON	
MINNESOTA		LOS ANGELES	

(continued)

Table 3-1 *(continued)*

English	Sign	English	Sign
NEW YORK		MIAMI	
TEXAS		PITTSBURGH	

Signin' the Sign

Tim is telling Angie about a road trip he and Buddy are taking to visit friends in several states.

Tim: Buddy and I are taking a trip.
Sign: B-U-D-D-Y (point) ME — TRAVEL — WILL

Angie: Wow! Sounds like a fun time.
Sign: WOW — SEEMS FUN

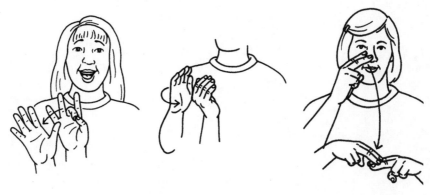

Tim: We're going to Texas, California, and Colorado.
Sign: US TRAVEL WHERE — TEXAS CALIFORNIA COLORADO

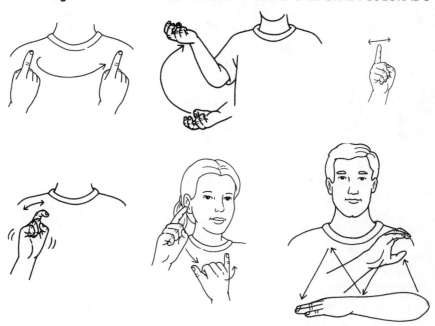

Angie:	Will you see Chip?
Sign:	C-H-I-P SEE — Q

Tim:	Yes, Chip's in LA.
Sign:	YES — C-H-I-P LA

Describing locations

Locations add the details to what you're signing. Details are the key to clear and precise conversation. The following location descriptions will help:

BRIDGE

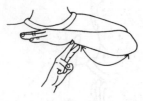

LAKE

CORNER

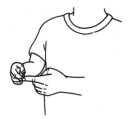

TREE

MOUNTAIN

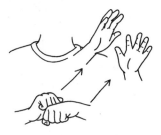

RIVER

FLOWERS

GRASS

FOUNTAIN

Signin' the Sign

Dee and Ted are in Japan. They're in awe of the beautiful country and are sharing their feelings about the experience.

Dee: The trees are beautiful in Japan.
Sign: JAPAN — TREES — BEAUTIFUL

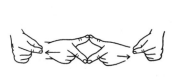 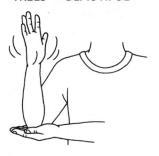 

Ted: The mountains are so high.
Sign: MOUNTAINS HIGH

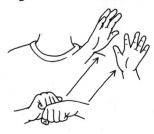

Dee: There are so many rivers.
Sign: RIVERS — MANY

 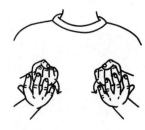

Fun & Games

Look at the various Signs given and try to find those words in the following puzzle. The answers are in Appendix A.

1.

2.

3.

4.

5.

6.

7.

(continued)

W	K	E	E	S	S	O
F	L	Y	M	T	U	C
R	D	F	Q	U	A	I
A	N	G	R	Y	I	X
N	A	M	E	X	M	E
C	E	Y	B	O	O	M
E	H	E	L	L	O	F

Chapter 4

Getting to Know You: Asking Questions and Making Small Talk

. . . .

In This Chapter

▶ Asking questions in conversation

▶ Talking about family and friends

▶ Getting addresses and phone numbers

▶ Talking about where you work

▶ Understanding pronouns and possessives

. . . .

Hearing people get to know each other by asking questions and making small talk. ASL is no different. You start with the basics and build from there. This chapter shows you how to converse with your family and friends in the silent language by giving you the Signs for various questions, for getting addresses and phone numbers, and by letting you know how to use pronouns instead of names. Showing ownership (possessives) is covered, too. Making small talk needs questions, Signs, and some basic information on talking about family, yourself and, of course, home and work. This chapter is a sure bet to get you signing in no time.

Signing Key Questions: Six Ws, One H

When you want to sign a question, you simply put the question word at the end of the sentence — words such as **who, what, when, where, which, why,** and **how.** In this section, we explain these key Signs first, and then we show you how to ask questions, putting those question Signs at the end of the sentence.

After you sign your question, as a rule, you sign the manual question mark repeatedly — the manual question mark you use at the **end of a sentence** is shown below.

Question mark (end of sentence)

Throughout this book, the letter **Q** follows all ASL examples and dialogues that are questions. Use the end of sentence manual question mark when you see the letter Q in this book.

You also have the option of placing the question mark at the beginning of the sentence.

Question mark (beginning of sentence)

As you sign the question word, lean forward a little, look inquisitive, scrunch your eyebrows together, and tilt your head to one side.

Your dominant hand — the one that you write with — does the action.

Always maintain eye contact. That way, you and the other person can make sure that you understand one another.

You sign the following inquiry words at the beginning or at the end of a sentence.

Who? With your dominant hand, place your thumb on your chin and let your index finger wiggle from the joint. The other three fingers curl under.

What? Put your hands outward in front of you, with elbows bent and palms up. Shake your hands back and forth towards each other.

Where? Hold up the index finger of your dominant hand as if you're indicating "number one;" shake it side to side.

When? Put both of your index fingers together at a 90-degree angle at the tips. Your dominant index finger then makes a full circle around the passive index finger and returns to the starting position.

Which? Make both hands into fists with your thumbs pointing up; alternate each fist in an up-and-down movement.

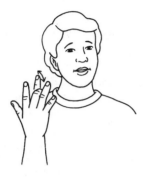

Why? Touch the side of your forehead with the fingers of your dominant hand; extend your thumb and pinky (in the Y sign) as you bring your hand down, middle three fingers in, to chest level.

How? With fingers pointing downward and backs of fingers and knuckles touching, roll hands inward to your chest and up so that the pinky sides of your hands are touching.

Check out the following examples of short questions:

English: Who is going?
Sign: GOING WHO Q

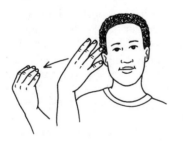

English: What do you mean?
Sign: MEAN WHAT Q (The word "you" is implied because you're talking to that person already.)

Signin' the Sign

 Virginia and Mark are roommates. It's Saturday morning, and they're drinking coffee and signing about what they have planned for the day.

Mark: Are you working today?
Sign: TODAY — WORKING YOU Q

Virginia: Yes, for two hours.
Sign: YES — TWO HOURS — SHORT (This signed answer can be translated to mean "I am only working briefly.")

Mark: I'm going to the movies.
Sign: MOVIES — GO ME

Virginia: May I join you?
Sign: JOIN (you) ME Q (**Note:** the word "you" is a directional word to be signed toward the person you're joining.)

Mark: Of course.
Sign: OF COURSE

Talking about Yourself

This section helps you to confidently share information about yourself and your family. Understanding another person's Signs is one thing, but responding to them is another. You already know all the ins and outs of who your relatives are and where you live and work, so here's where you find the most commonly used Signs to convey that information.

Family and friends

Describing your family is one way to tell someone about yourself. Using the common Signs in Table 4-1 can make your eccentric family seem almost normal.

Table 4-1		Family Members	
English	*Sign*	*English*	*Sign*
FATHER		MOTHER	

(continued)

Table 4-1 *(continued)*

English	Sign	English	Sign
SON		DAUGHTER	
BROTHER		SISTER	
AUNT		UNCLE	

English	Sign	English	Sign
MALE COUSIN		FEMALE COUSIN	
FAMILY			

Signs for some other members of your family, such as grandparents and in-laws, are a bit trickier. To talk about your **grandparents** or your **grandchildren,** fingerspell G-R-A-N-D and then sign the person.

In-laws are easy enough: Sign the person and then sign **law.**

Also, to sign **stepbrother, stepsister, stepmother,** or **stepfather,** hold your hand straight out in front your chest and, with your thumb pointing straight up and index finger pointing forward, shake your hand back and forth; then sign the person. It sort of looks like you're pointing at someone with a very shaky hand.

Sign a **half sibling** by expressing the manual "½" and then brother or sister.

Take a look at these examples:

English: Is this your sister?
Sign: SISTER — YOURS Q

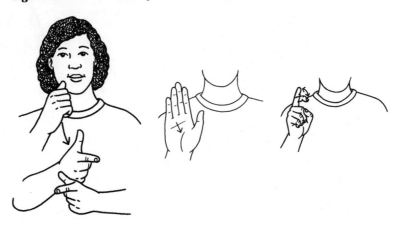

English: No, she's my sister-in-law.
Sign: NO — SISTER LAW — MINE HER (point)

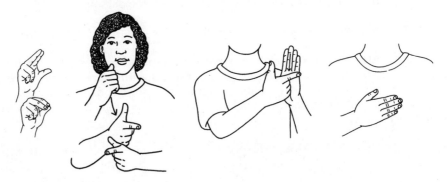

English: He is my half brother.
Sign: MY 1-2 (as in ½) BROTHER HIM (point)

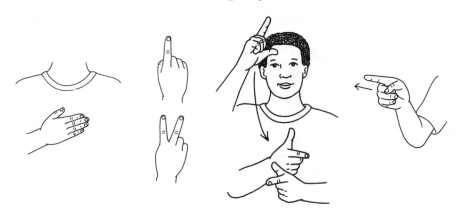

To sign a school or work friend, simply sign the word and then sign **friend.**
You may signify a good friend, a close friend, or a friend who's like a brother
or sister by signing friend with more intensity. You can also indicate that
close friends are **like two peas in a pod** by signing crossed fingers — it looks
the same as when you cross your fingers to mean "good luck" or "I hope so."

Relating where you live and work

Giving others information about your workplace and home is easy — the
information is already in your memory. Signing this info to others is a snap,
but be careful because many other eyes can see what you sign.

Giving addresses and phone numbers

Exchanging addresses and phone numbers is a great way to make friends
with other Signers. Asking for repeats is okay; everyone does it in both
English and Sign. You fingerspell most of this information; however, north,
south, east, and west have Signs — see Chapter 10. You can abbreviate the
following:

- ✔ **Avenue:** A-V-E
- ✔ **Circle:** C-R
- ✔ **Drive:** D-R
- ✔ **Street:** S-T
- ✔ **Apartment:** A-P-T
- ✔ **Way:** W-Y

Prominent cities may have *name Signs* (see Chapter 3). For less prominent cities, fingerspell the name. Deaf people will show you a local Sign if it exists. Quite often, you sign cities that have two-word names by using the first letter of each word. As a general rule, sign cities the way the Deaf do — as they say, when in Rome. . . .

You sign zip codes with your palm facing outward. Sign all five numbers in succession.

Sign street addresses by fingerspelling the street name and then signing the house number — keeping your palm facing the addressee. Sign the city's name next, but only when you're sure that the addressee understands the Sign; otherwise, fingerspell the city's name.

When you sign phone numbers, all numbers face the addressee — outward. If you're not sure that the information you're giving is clear, sign an area code by making parentheses with both index fingers and then signing the numbers. More often, though, area codes don't require the parentheses, just sign L-D (for long distance) before you give the number. Signing the suffix part of phone numbers doesn't follow any set rule. Some people fingerspell all four numbers in succession while others break it up into two sets of two numbers. For instance, if the last four numbers of a phone number are 1212, you can sign them as 1, 2, 1, 2 or 12, 12. You don't need to worry about putting a hyphen between the numbers like you would if you were writing the number down.

The following Signs may help you, too:

DOWNTOWN

COUNTRY/SUBURB

CITY

TOWN

STREET

PHONE

LONG DISTANCE

ADDRESS

CELL PHONE

PAGER

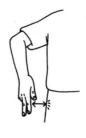

CALL (SUMMONS)

Signin' the Sign

Donna is moving to Chicago. Mike is hoping that the two of them can stay in touch; Donna feels the same way. Mike wants to get her new address so that he can write to her.

Mike: Where are you moving?
Sign: MOVING YOU — WHERE Q

 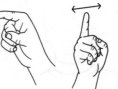 

Donna: Chicago. Will you write?
Sign: CHICAGO — LETTER ME — YOU Q

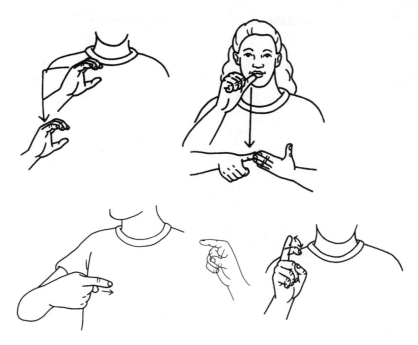

Mike: Yes, what's your address?
Sign: YES — ADDRESS YOURS — WHAT Q

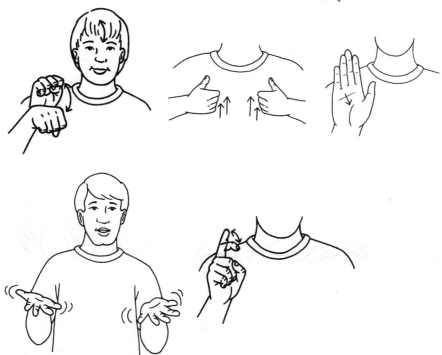

Donna: 171 Anywhere Lane, 98765.
Sign: A-N-Y-W-H-E-R-E L-A-N-E — 1-7-1— 9-8-7-6-5

Mike: Thanks. Phone me when you arrive.
Sign: THANKS — ARRIVE YOU — PHONE ME

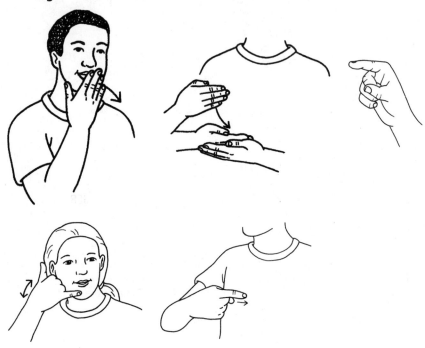

Jabbering about your job

When you want to tell someone the name of where you work, you usually do it by fingerspelling. If the name of your company is an acronym, you finger-spell that as well. Few places have name Signs that are understood by every-one. However, when sharing info about your profession, be it your job title or what your job entails, you can usually use Signs. Table 4-2 lists just a few of the many job Signs used today.

Table 4-2		Job Signs	
English	*Sign*	*English*	*Sign*
BOSS		COOK	
INTERPRETER		MANAGER	
DOCTOR		ACCOUNTANT	

(continued)

Table 4-2 (continued)

English	Sign	English	Sign
POLICE		TEACHER	
PRESIDENT		TREASURER	
SECRETARY		VICE PRESIDENT	

English	Sign	English	Sign
MECHANIC		SALESPERSON	
ASSISTANT		LAWYER	
SERVER			

Signin' the Sign

 Juanita and Tim are seated next to each other at a dinner party hosted by Tom, a mutual friend. They strike up a casual conversation.

Tim: Hi, I'm Tim, Tom's accountant.
Sign: HI — T-I-M ME — ACCOUNTANT FOR T-O-M

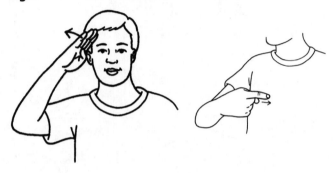

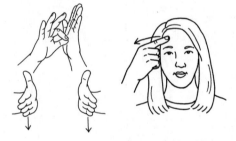

Juanita: I'm Juanita. Nice to meet you.
Sign: J-U-A-N-I-T-A ME — NICE MEET YOU

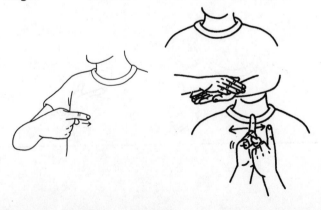

Tim: Do you work with Tom at Bailey & Sons?
Sign: BAILEY & SONS — T-O-M YOU — WORK TOGETHER Q

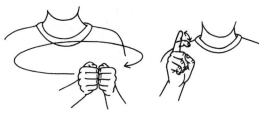

Juanita: Yes, I'm vice-president of marketing.
Sign: YES — MARKETING — V.P. — ME

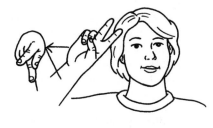

Tim: What an interesting job.
Sign: JOB — INTERESTING — TRUE

Juanita: I sure meet a lot of different people.
Sign: PEOPLE — DIFFERENT — MEET ME

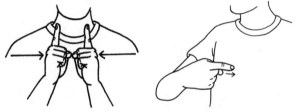

Using Possessives and Pronouns

In the course of getting to know someone, especially when you're both asking questions about each other, you'll find that it's probably easier to use pronouns. Using pronouns in Sign is the same as in English; you need to refer to a noun before you use a pronoun. Of course, if you're using a pronoun to indicate someone or something nearby, you can point to that person or thing as you sign.

You may also use possessives during your conversation. Show possession by indicating whom you are talking about, what is being possessed, and then an open palm facing the person. You can also use proper nouns (a person's name) to discuss possessives. Fingerspell the name of the person and then point to the item you're talking about and sign a question mark. For example, suppose that you're signing with someone and you want to know if the coat on the hook belongs to Tony. Fingerspell T-O-N-Y, point to the coat, and sign a question mark.

If you're signing *with* Tony, point to the object or fingerspell it if it's not in view, look at Tony, sign toward him with an open palm, and then make a question mark. You've now asked him "Is that yours?" Remember to keep your eyebrows up and wear an inquisitive look.

Table 4-3 gives a list of pronouns that refer to people, and it also gives you the Signs for the regular and the possessive pronouns. As you can see, some Signs are used for more than one pronoun. Simple sentences can follow English word order. Put the possessive pronoun Sign before or after the person or thing you're signing; the order doesn't matter. For example:

English: My dog.
Sign: DOG MINE or MY DOG

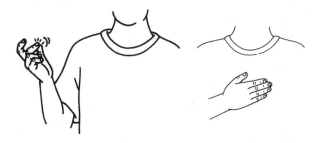

Table 4-3	Personal and Possessive Pronouns		
Pronoun	*Sign*	*Possessive*	*Sign*
I, ME		MY, MINE	
HE		HIS	
SHE		HERS	

(continued)

Table 4-3 (continued)

Pronoun	Sign	Possessive	Sign
YOU (singular)		YOUR, YOURS (singular)	
YOU (plural)		YOUR, YOURS (plural)	
WE, US		OUR, OURS	
THEY, THEM		THEIR, THEIRS	
IT		ITS	

As a group, four little pronouns — **this, that, these,** and **those** — get a big name, *demonstrative pronouns.* But you don't really need to know the name, just the Signs, which are in Table 4-4.

Table 4-4	Demonstrative Pronouns		
Pronoun	*Sign*	*Plural*	*Sign*
THIS		THESE	
THAT		THOSE	

Sign the pronoun **that** by pointing to your subject with your dominant hand in the **Y** shape and bent at the wrist. Sign **this, these,** and **those** by pointing to the subject or subjects.

Sign singular possessives by holding your hand, palm outward, toward the person to whom you're referring. Sign plural possessives the same way, but also move your hand from side to side in front of each person in a sort of sweeping motion.

The following sentences can give you some practice with pronouns and possessives:

English: He is rich.
Sign: RICH HIM

English: He has money.
Sign: MONEY HIS

English: She is wise.
Sign: WISE HER

English: She has wisdom.
Sign: WISDOM HERS

English: They have gold.
Sign: GOLD HAVE THEM

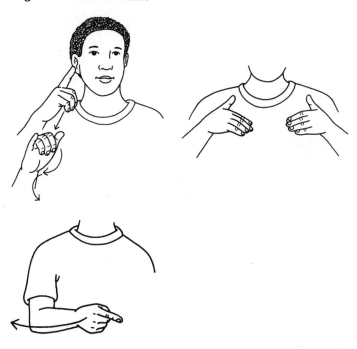

English: The gold is theirs.
Sign: GOLD THEIRS

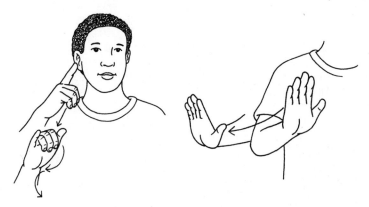

Fun & Games

Match the Signs with the words. Feel free to go back through this chapter to find them. Your goal isn't necessarily to get the Signs all correct but to get used to using them.

1. uncle _____
2. teacher _____
3. his _____
4. call _____
5. which _____
6. sister _____
7. mother _____
8. work _____
9. city _____
10. my/mine _____
11. why _____
12. server _____

c.

f.

g.

d.

a.

h.

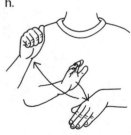

b.

e.

i.

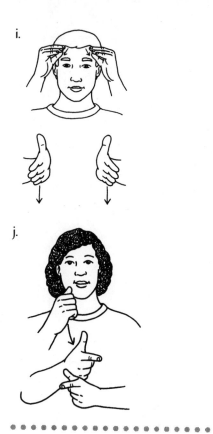

j.

k.

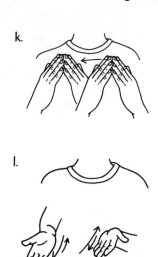

l.

Chapter 5

Food: The Whole Enchilada

. . . .

In This Chapter

▶ Munching morning, noon, and night

▶ Dining in restaurants

▶ Enjoying ethnic foods

▶ Expanding sentences

▶ Going to the grocery

. . . .

*W*hen dining out with Deaf people, who love to wine and dine like anyone else, you might want to ask them what's good on the menu, but you don't know how. This chapter covers signing three squares, dining out and ordering drinks, and finding sales and specials in the grocery store.

Eating Three Squares a Day

When you're lucky enough to get an invitation to join other Signers for brunch, take along these Signs to get you through the event. Here we go over Signs of breakfast, lunch, and dinner plus everything you'll see on the table — except your elbows. Before you dive into a dish of delights for any meal, check out Table 5-1 for a list of some necessary tools.

Table 5-1		Utensils and Dishes	
English	*Sign*	*English*	*Sign*
BOWL		CUP	
FORK		GLASS (drinking)	
KNIFE		NAPKIN	
PLATE		SPOON	

These next sentences help you to see Sign in action. Here's how to sign the words for what you'll need at the table. A good host not only knows when to use the salad fork but also how to sign it. To sign **place setting**, sign **fork, knife,** and **spoon.** A great way to remember how to make the Signs for tableware is pretty simple. What you do with the objects relates to the Signs. For example, **napkin** is a wiping motion on the mouth; **spoon** uses a scooping motion; **fork** has a stabbing motion; **knife** has a cutting motion.

English: I need another place setting, please.
Sign: PLEASE — KNIFE FORK SPOON — NEED ME

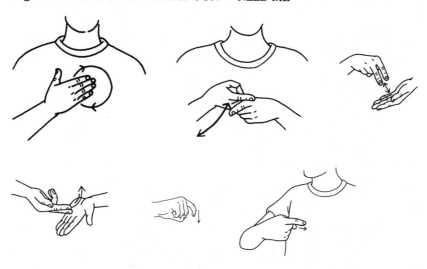

English: The plate and glass are broken.
Sign: PLATE — GLASS — BROKEN

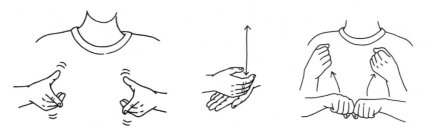

English: I need three bowls.
Sign: THREE BOWLS — NEED ME

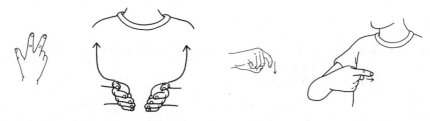

English: The napkin is dirty.
Sign: NAPKIN — DIRTY

Table 5-2 shows you how to sign meal-related words.

Table 5-2	Mealtime
English	*Sign*
BREAKFAST	
LUNCH	

English	Sign
DINNER	
FOOD	
EAT	
HUNGRY	

If you want to show **gorging,** sign **food** with both hands alternately putting food in your mouth while your cheeks are puffed out or your mouth is wide open. The faster you sign, the more you gorge. To sign **starving,** just sign **hungry** faster, open your mouth a little, and look hungry.

Having breakfast

Because breakfast is the most important meal of the day, the signs for breakfast foods are the most important ones of the day. The signs in Table 5-3 certainly help at the breakfast bar or at the breakfast table.

Table 5-3		Breakfast Foods	
English	**Sign**	**English**	**Sign**
BACON		CEREAL	
EGGS		SAUSAGE	
TOAST			

Even if you're still half asleep, you won't have any problems figuring out most of these Signs: The Sign for **bacon** mimics the waviness of a fried strip; **toast** lets you know that the bread is browned on both sides; **cereal** is the crunchy stuff you chew. Use the common abbreviations for **orange juice** and sign the letters **O** and **J** to convey this popular breakfast beverage (the Cheat Sheet at the front of this book has the manual alphabet). Get going on practicing your early-morning skills with the following examples:

English: I want eggs, not cereal.
Sign: EGGS WANT — CEREAL NOT — ME

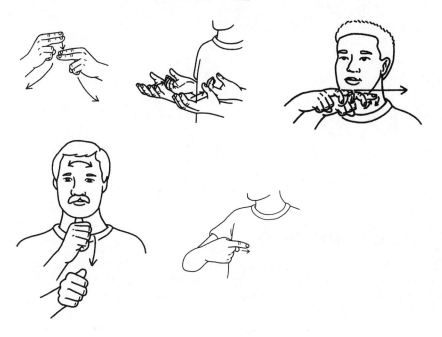

English: The orange juice is cold.
Sign: COLD O-J

English: I'll have sausage and eggs.
Sign: SAUSAGE — EGGS — HAVE ME

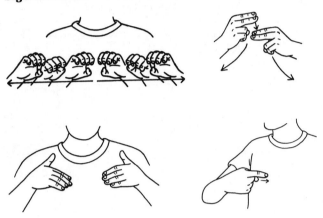

Eating lunch

Doing lunch with friends is at your fingertips. The set of Signs in Table 5-4 can hold you through the afternoon — just don't get too excited about signing these items, or you may end up eating them all in one sitting!

Table 5-4		Lunch Items	
English	*Sign*	*English*	*Sign*
BURGER		CHEESE	

English	Sign	English	Sign
SODA		FRENCH FRIES	
PIZZA		SALAD	
SANDWICH			

To order a hamburger, you imitate the motions of making a patty, but for other lunch Signs, you use the manual alphabet (shown on the Cheat Sheet at the front of this book). For example, **French fries** is the letter **F** repeated, and you sign **pizza** by bending your index and middle fingers and then making a manual **Z.** Follow these examples:

English: I'm hungry, and it's time for lunch.
Sign: NOW TIME — NOON FOOD — HUNGRY ME

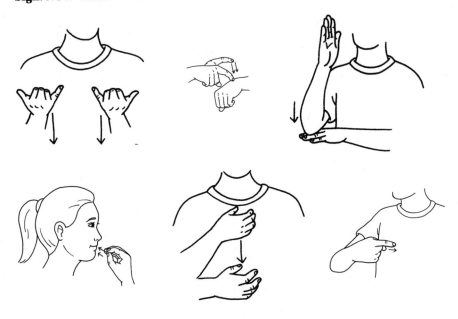

English: I'd like a cheeseburger and fries.
Sign: CHEESEBURGER — FRIES — LIKE ME

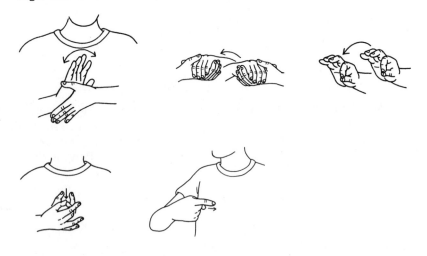

English: The soda is cold.
Sign: SODA — COLD

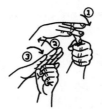

English: I want a sandwich and salad for lunch.
Sign: NOON FOOD — SANDWICH — SALAD — WANT ME

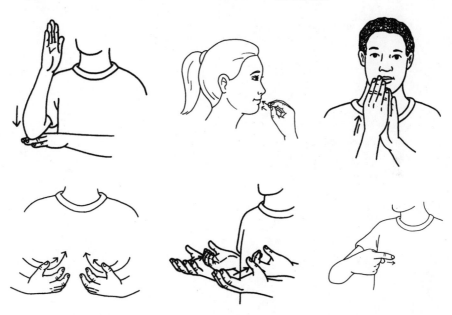

Signin' the Sign

Several co-workers are going to lunch and are discussing what they're in the mood to eat. Here's what they each decide.

Dee: I'm hungry; I want a hamburger, french fries, and a soda.

Sign: HUNGRY ME — HAMBURGER FRENCH FRIES SODA — WANT ME

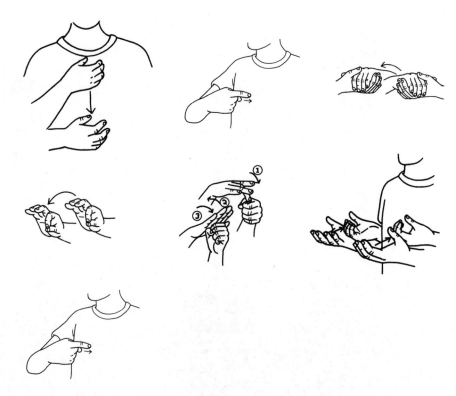

Ted: I want a fish sandwich and water.

Sign: FISH SANDWICH — WATER — WANT ME

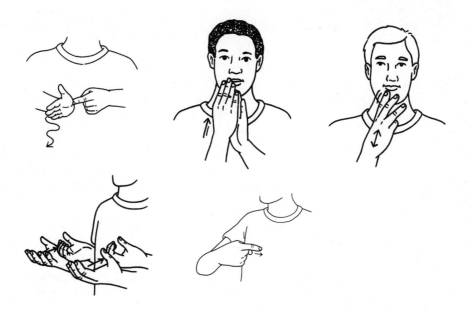

Denni: I want breakfast: sausage, eggs, toast, and milk.
Sign: MORNING FOOD — SAUSAGE EGGS TOAST MILK —
WANT ME

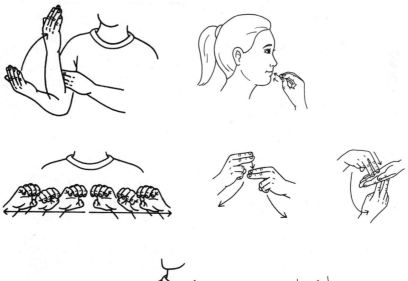

Wanda: They have chicken.
Sign: CHICKEN — HAVE THEM (point)

  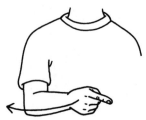

Enjoying dinner

Supper is ready, and so are you. Putting the evening meal into conversation is a piece of cake. Follow the Signs in Table 5-5, and you'll say a mouthful. (The Signs for drinks are coming up in the "Drinking for the young and old" section.)

Table 5-5		Dinner Terms	
English	**Sign**	**English**	**Sign**
BREAD		CHICKEN	
FISH		FULL	

English	Sign	English	Sign
HAM		POTATO	
SOUP		SPAGHETTI	
STEAK			

Fortunately, **chicken, fish,** and **pig** are signed like the food they provide. If you want to order steak or beef, you can use the same Sign for either one.

Signing how you want it cooked is a breeze; just use the manual alphabet and give your hand a little shake: M, M-W, and W-D. If you want your steak rare, fingerspell R-A-R-E. You may also sign it **cook** and **short.** Short is signed like knife, but it uses a single motion (see the section on utensils earlier in the chapter for more on how to sign knife).

Don't sign rare with a shaken **R** — to the untrained eye it could be mistaken for "restroom" or the direction "right."

Here are some dinner-related sentences to give you practice:

English: Soup and bread were served.
Sign: FINISH — SOUP — BREAD — SERVE

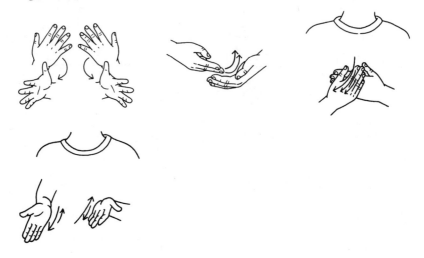

Finish at the beginning of a sentence adds past tense to the whole sentence. (See Chapter 2 for more information on signing in past tense.)

English: Chicken and spaghetti are on special.
Sign: SPECIAL — WHAT — CHICKEN — SPAGHETTI

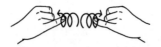

English: The steak is rare.
Sign: STEAK — R-A-R-E

English: I'd like a potato with my fish.
Sign: MY FISH — POTATO TOGETHER — WANT ME

English: I'm full.
Sign: FULL ME

Dining Out

Everyone enjoys going out to restaurants from time to time. Take a look at the signs in Table 5-6, which you can use no matter what type of restaurant you go to. *Bon appetit!*

Deaf people usually point out to the server what they want on the menu. If you're dining out with Deaf people, don't try to take control when ordering. They've probably been eating in restaurants long before they met you.

Table 5-6	Words for Dining Out		
English	*Sign*	*English*	*Sign*
ORDER		RESERVATION	
RESTAURANT		SERVER/ WAITER/ WAITRESS	

The preceding signs are pretty descriptive whether you're filling the table

Ethnic food around town

Restaurant row is just down the street. Many Deaf people enjoy these establishments, and you'd like to enjoy both the food and the company. These food Signs in Table 5-7 are just the thing to get you going — come and get it!

ASL doesn't have established Signs for ethnic foods. If the grub is popular, you may see a variety of ways to sign it if there isn't already an established Sign from its country of origin. In the southwestern part of the United States, Mexican food is popular, and Mexican Sign Language for this ethnic food is pretty well established in the border states.

Table 5-7	Ethnic Foods		
English	**Sign**	**English**	**Sign**
LASAGNA		SUSHI	
TACO		TORTILLA	
TOSTADA			

The preceding signs are pretty descriptive whether you're filling a taco shell, shaping a tortilla, or layering lasagna. The following sentences will work up an appetite for any eager Signer:

English: We will eat dinner at a restaurant.
Sign: RESTAURANT — EVENING FOOD — EAT THERE — WE WILL

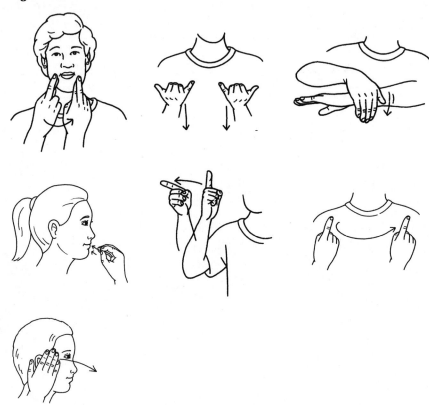

English: I like egg rolls.
Sign: EGG R-O-L-L-S — LIKE ME

English: Tostadas are cheap.
Sign: TOSTADA — CHEAP

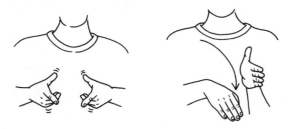

English: She likes tortillas.
Sign: TORTILLAS — SHE LIKES

Don't forget the drinks!

When dining out or going for a night on the town, drinks are often a big part of the occasion. Table 5-8 can help you when ordering common beverages.

Table 5-8		Common Beverages	
English	*Sign*	*English*	*Sign*
BEER		COFFEE	

(continued)

Table 5-8 *(continued)*

English	Sign	English	Sign
WHISKEY/SHOT		WINE	
SODA/COLA		MILK	
WATER		TEA	

English: We need ice.
Sign: I-C-E — NEED US

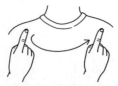

English: The water is warm.
Sign: WATER — WARM

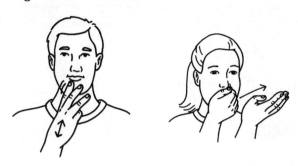

English: I need a glass for my beer.
Sign: BEER GLASS — NEED ME

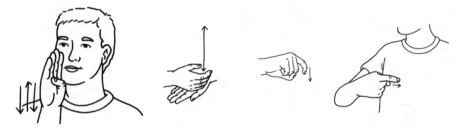

English: The coffee is strong.
Sign: COFFEE — STRONG

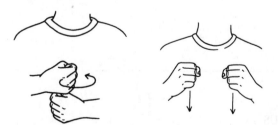

Signin' the Sign

Belinda, Della, Dee, and Denni are out on the town. Belinda wants to propose a toast and is making sure that everyone has a drink when the waitress approaches.

Belinda: What would you all like to drink?
Sign: DRINK — WANT WHAT Q

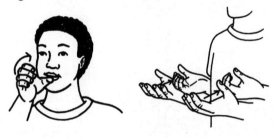

Dee: A glass of red wine.
Sign: RED WINE

Della: Just a soda with ice.
Sign: SODA — I-C-E

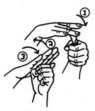

Denni: A cold beer.
Sign: COLD BEER

Complex Sentences

Complex sentences in Sign can be explained in two ways. First, a complex sentence occurs when a *circumstance* is added to a sentence. A circumstance is a phrase that usually starts with a *conditional word,* such as "if," or "suppose."

You sign the conditional word while raising your eyebrows but then follow with the rest of the conditional phrase and sentence with your eyebrows back down in their normal position.

A complex sentence also occurs when a sentence uses phrases that show a relationship between two ideas that refer to the same subject. When signing this type of complex sentence, first refer to the subject and then use a pronoun, such as "himself," "herself," or "itself" before continuing with the rest of the idea. Following are some examples of these two complex sentence types:

English: If you order beer, I'll order wine.
Sign: IF BEER ORDER YOU — WINE ORDER ME

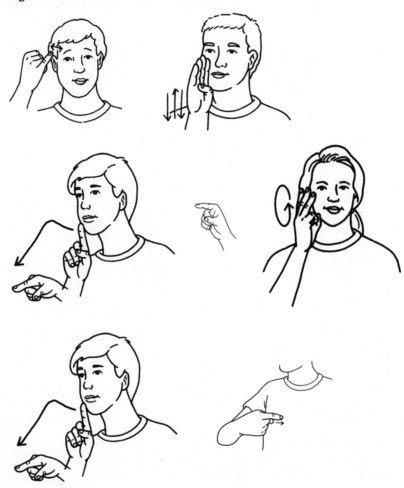

English: You can't eat your lasagna because you have no fork.
Sign: LASAGNA — EAT YOU CAN'T — WHY — FORK HAVE YOU NOT

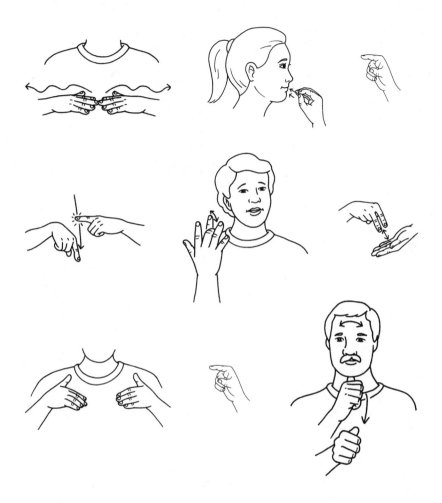

Attention, Shoppers!

Shopping made simple — that's what you'll find when you do it in Sign. This section gives you a handle on grocery stores and specials.

Signing specialty stores

Everyone at one time or another goes to market. You'll be the guru of groceries, hands down, when using the Signs from Table 5-9.

Table 5-9		Types of Stores	
English	*Sign*	*English*	*Sign*
BAKERY (BREAD STORE)		BUTCHER (MEAT STORE)	
CONVENIENCE STORE (7-11 STORE)		DISCOUNT STORE (ONE DOLLAR STORE)	
GROCERY (FOOD STORE)			

English: I went to the butcher's.
Sign: FINISH — MEAT STORE — GO ME

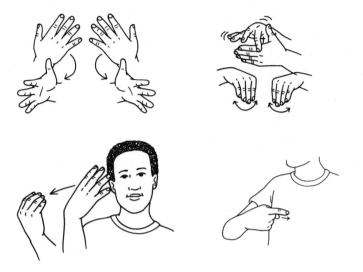

English: The bakery smells good.
Sign: BREAD STORE — SMELLS DELICIOUS

English: The grocery store is open.
Sign: FOOD STORE — OPEN

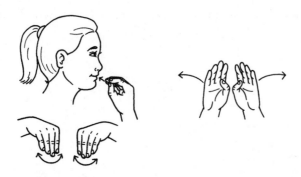

What's on special?

Few things are more satisfying than saving money when you're shopping for groceries. Signing specials from the marketplace, like those in Table 5-10, will give you the upper hand as you finger your way through the fruit. Note that some signs mean several words, as in "two for the price of one."

Table 5-10		Sale Ad Words	
English	*Sign*	*English*	*Sign*
SAVE		SPEND/BUY	
SALE/SELL		BARGAIN/CHEAP	

English	Sign	
COUPON		

English: The meat is on sale today.
Sign: TODAY — MEAT SALE

   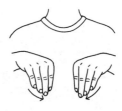

English: You can buy two steaks for the price of one.
Sign: TWO STEAKS — PAY — ONLY ONE

 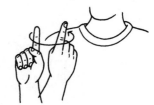

English: I saved money.
Sign: FINISH — MONEY SAVE ME

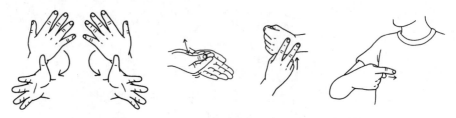

English: You spent too much.
Sign: FINISH — SPEND — (implied YOU) TOO MUCH

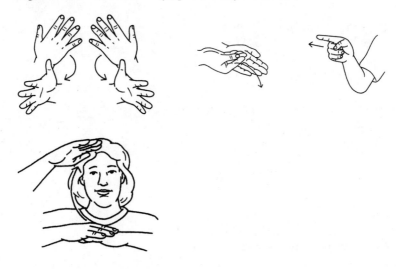

Let me sell you on this: A good way to sign "two for the price of one" is **buy two pay one.** "Coupon" can be signed by signing **discount** and then making a small square in the area with your index fingers.

Fun & Games

Sign the following words. You can look back in the chapter for help.

1. Sign three different utensils (worth 3 pts.).

2. Sign three different types of beverages (worth 3 pts.).

3. Sign one Italian food (worth 1 pt.).

4. Sign one Mexican food (worth 1 pt.).

5. Sign the words "full" and "hungry" (worth 2 pts.).

6. Sign the words "eggs" and "cereal" (worth 2 pts.).

7. Sign the word "salad" (worth 1 pt.).

Fourteen total points are possible. Let's see how you did:

10–13:   Thumbs up!

6–9:   You're getting there!

1–5:   Keep practicing!

Chapter 6

Shopping Made Easy

· ·

In This Chapter

▶ Clothing in Sign

▶ Coloring your wardrobe

▶ Comparing costs

· ·

Signing and shopping fit together like hand and glove. This chapter focuses on fashions, colors, and seasons in Sign. Comparing prices and money Signs are thrown in, too — at no cost to you.

Clothes for All Seasons

Dapper duds are all the rage. These Signs show you how to ask for and get your garb in any season because everyone loves a well-dressed Signer. Table 6-1 talks fabric. Although many fabrics are fingerspelled, here are some fabrics that are signed.

Fabric Signs bear a strong resemblance to what they represent. For example, **leather** is similar to cowhide, and **cotton** is like tearing apart a cotton ball.

Table 6-1		Fabrics	
English	*Sign*	*English*	*Sign*
COTTON		FABRIC	
LEATHER			

These words are the basics for all your clothing needs. **Wear** is signed the same as **use**, so don't worry that they look the same. **Clothes** is the same Sign as **costume** — try that on for size!

WEAR   **CLOTHES**

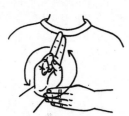   

The winter look

Changing with the seasons is no problem. Winter wear Signs are cool because they look like what they are. Check them out in Table 6-2.

Table 6-2		Winter Clothing	
English	*Sign*	*English*	*Sign*
BOOTS		COAT	
GLOVES		HAT	
LONG/THERMAL UNDERWEAR		SCARF	

There are a variety of Signs for gloves because there are different kinds of gloves. Either way, mimic putting on a pair of gloves. Mittens can be signed by making an outline of your thumb and four fingers with the index finger of your passive hand. Mittens are not as common as gloves, so if people don't understand you, you can always rely on fingerspelling.

Hat and **scarf** are simple: Sign them like you're putting them on.

Boots are signed like the action of pulling them on your legs. It seems women tend to sign boot on the arm, and men seem to sign it on the leg. (This isn't a rule, only one observation.)

Try these sentences on for size:

English: Wear your coat.
Sign: YOUR COAT WEAR

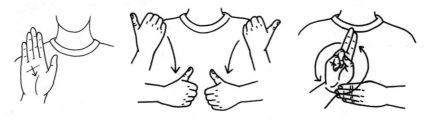

English: The scarf is white.
Sign: SCARF WHITE

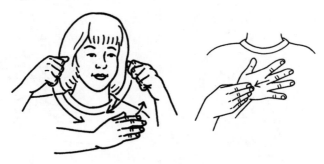

English: Are these your gloves?
Sign: GLOVES YOURS Q

Now, it's time to go under cover. Most of these Signs are signed to look like what they represent. Anything slinky or kinky is fingerspelled. **Men's briefs** can be signed like **panties; men's boxers** can be, too. You may often see **men's and women's long johns** expressed by signing "long" and then fingerspelling J-O-H-N-S. **T-shirt** is signed with the manual handshape T then shirt. Take a look at Table 6-3 for clarification.

Table 6-3	Underwear		
English	*Sign*	*English*	*Sign*
PANTIES		BRA	
UNDERWEAR (men)		T-SHIRT	

Fall fashion

You'll have no trouble with fall fashions when you know the basic Signs (see Table 6-4) for cool weather wear.

Table 6-4	Cool Clothing		
English	*Sign*	*English*	*Sign*
BELT		DRESS	
HIGH HEELS		PANTS/SLACKS	
SHIRT		SHOES	
SOCKS		SWEATER	

Be cool. Practice these sentences that feature cool-weather wear:

English: Your dress is pretty.
Sign: YOUR DRESS — PRETTY

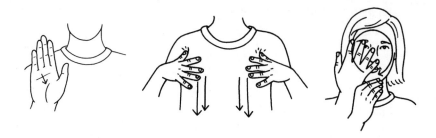

English: Her belt is leather.
Sign: HER BELT — LEATHER

English: If you wear pants, don't wear high heels.
Sign: IF PANTS USE — HIGH HEELS USE NOT

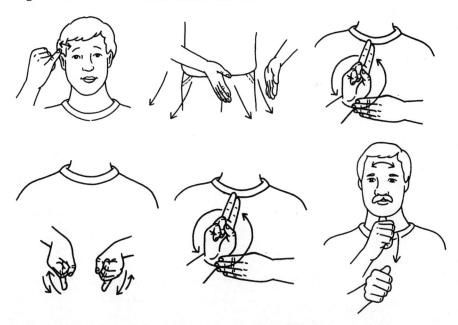

English: Where is my sweater?
Sign: MY SWEATER — WHERE Q

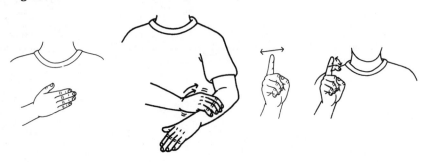

Spring style

Dressing for spring is a beautiful thing. The Signs in Table 6-5 show you how to fit in all the fashionable circles when the weather begins to warm up.

Table 6-5	Spring Apparel and Accessories		
English	*Sign*	*English*	*Sign*
BLOUSE		PURSE	
SKIRT		NYLONS	

English	Sign	English	Sign
TIE		UMBRELLA	
WALLET			

Spring into action and take a look at the following sentences:

English: Where's my umbrella?
Sign: MY UMBRELLA — WHERE Q

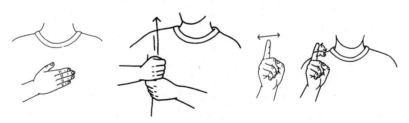

English: I want that skirt.
Sign: SKIRT — WANT ME

English: Where is my wallet?
Sign: MY WALLET — WHERE Q

English: If you wear a blouse, I'll wear a tie.
Sign: IF BLOUSE YOU WEAR — TIE ME WEAR

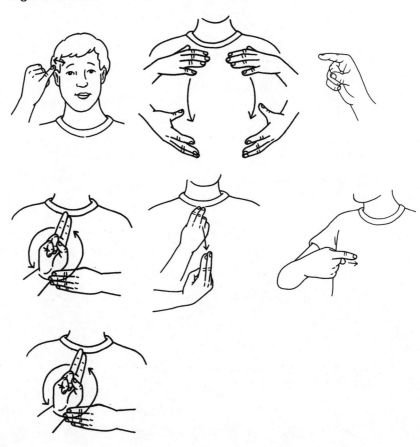

English: Her purse is nice.
Sign: HER PURSE —NICE

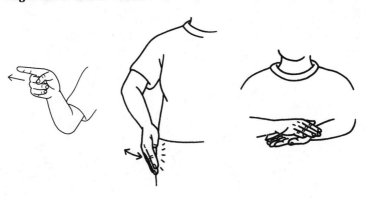

Summer suits

You can let everyone know your taste in summer wear with just a few bare-bones Signs. Table 6-6 gives you the hottest Signs for the coolest summer clothes.

Sunglasses are pretty much signed like glasses — just put the Sign for **sun** before **glasses.** A **two-piece swimsuit** for women is signed like **bra** and **panties;** a **one-piece swimsuit** is signed **one piece.** Men's **swimming trunks** are fingerspelled, or you can sign **shorts.** But if you're talking Speedos, sign it like panties.

Table 6-6		Summer Sizzlers	
English	*Sign*	*English*	*Sign*
SHORTS		SUNDRESS	

(continued)

Table 6-6 *(continued)*

English	Sign	English	Sign
SWIMSUIT (SWIM CLOTHES)		SUNGLASSES	

Now that you have the summer basics, try these sentences:

English: That's a pretty swimsuit.
Sign: SWIM CLOTHES — PRETTY

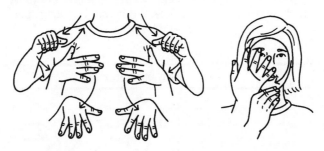

English: Where did you buy those sunglasses?
Sign: SUNGLASSES — BUY YOU — WHERE Q

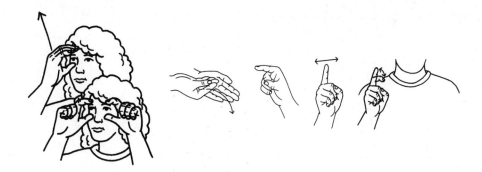

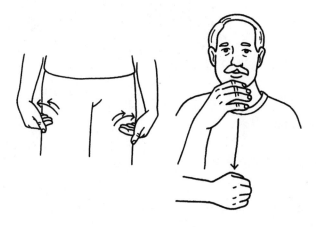

English: These shorts are old.
Sign: SHORTS (point) — OLD

English: When will the t-shirt shop open?
Sign: T-SHIRT SHOP — OPEN — WHEN Q

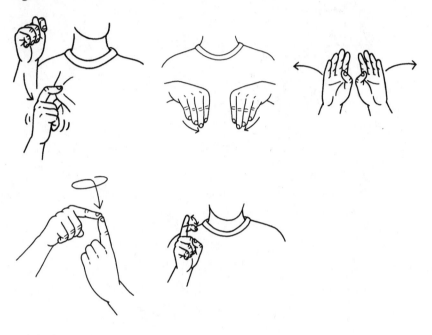

Clothing by color

Adding color to the canvas only brightens your repertoire of Sign. Time to bring it all home. This section gives you a start with your basic colors. Use the Signs in Table 6-7 to mix and match your way throughout the year. (Find the Sign for "white" in "The winter look," earlier in this chapter.)

Table 6-7	Common Colors		
English	*Sign*	*English*	*Sign*
BLACK		BLUE	

English	Sign	English	Sign
BROWN		GREEN	
ORANGE		PINK	
PURPLE		RED	
WHITE		YELLOW	

Following are some sentences that let you practice your newfound coloring skills:

English: Her dress is blue and white.
Sign: HER DRESS — BLUE WHITE

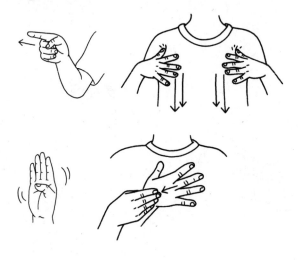

English: His tie is green.
Sign: HIS TIE — GREEN

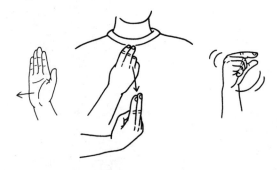

English: He wore a yellow cotton shirt.
Sign: FINISH — HE USE SHIRT — YELLOW COTTON

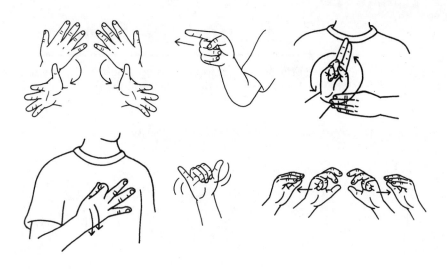

English: Her purse was black leather.
Sign: FINISH — HER PURSE — BLACK LEATHER

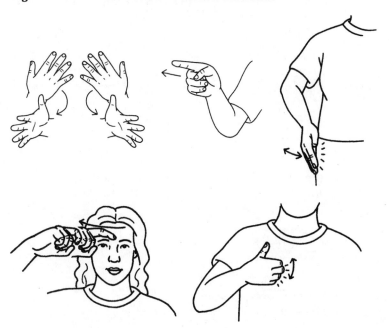

Signin' the Sign

Aurora and Dee are going shopping. There are many sales and they're looking for the best deals. Follow along as they move through the aisles.

Aurora: That blue dress is pretty.
Sign: BLUE DRESS — PRETTY

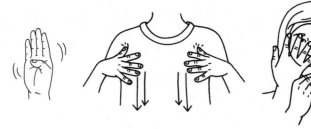

Dee: Those brown shoes are big.
Sign: BROWN SHOES — BIG

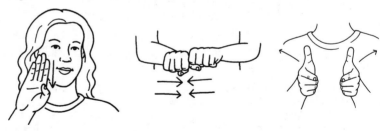

Aurora: Do you like the black slacks?
Sign: BLACK SLACKS — YOU LIKE Q

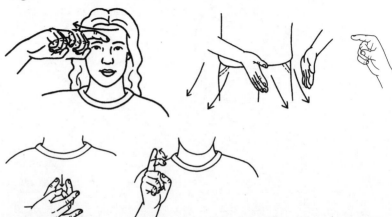

Dee: I like the leather pants.
Sign: LEATHER PANTS — LIKE ME

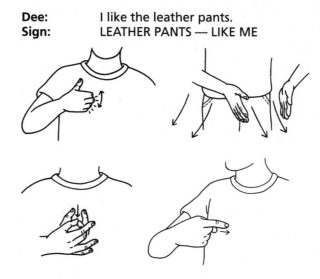

All about money

Now comes the not-so-fun part — paying for all your new items. But because you have to fork over the money, the Signs in Table 6-8 cover the variety of ways to pay for those purchases. Table 6-9 covers other money-related words.

Table 6-8		Payment Options	
English	*Sign*	*English*	*Sign*
ATM/DEBIT CARD		CASH	
CHARGE		CHECK	

(continued)

Table 6-8 (continued)

English	Sign	
CREDIT CARD		

Table 6-9   **Financial Words**

English	Sign	English	Sign
BANK		BILL (paper money)	
CENTS		CHANGE	
MONEY		PAY	

English: I'll pay with my credit card.
Sign: CREDIT CARD — PAY WILL ME

English: She wrote a $50 check.
Sign: FINISH — CHECK DOLLARS 5-0 — WRITE HER

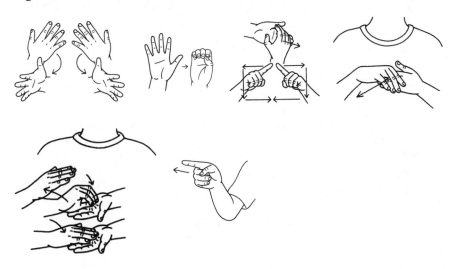

English: The bank gave me an ATM card.
Sign: A-T-M CARD — BANK — GIVE ME

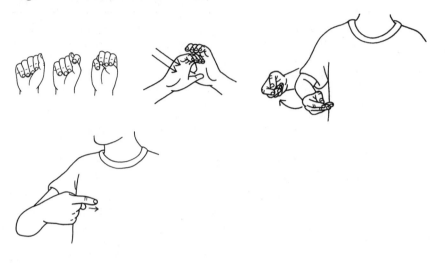

English: Those shoes cost $3.25.
Sign: SHOES — DOLLARS THREE — CENTS 25 — COST

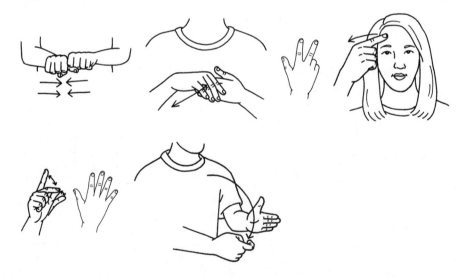

You can sign credit cards two different ways. The old way: Sign **credit card machine** as shown in Table 6-8. The new way: Outline a card shape and then show the motion of swiping it through a machine.

Signin' the Sign

 Robert and Krista are going clothes shopping. They like to save money, so they're doing some comparison shopping.

Robert: I'm buying new clothes.
Sign: NEW CLOTHES — BUY ME

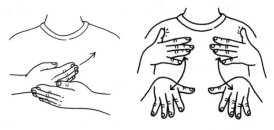

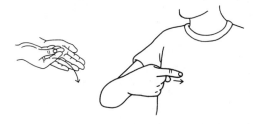

Krista: I didn't bring much money.
Sign: A LOT MONEY — HAVE ME — NOT

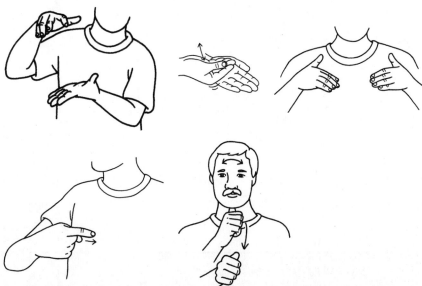

Robert: Buy a couple of blouses on sale.
Sign: TWO BLOUSES — SALE — BUY

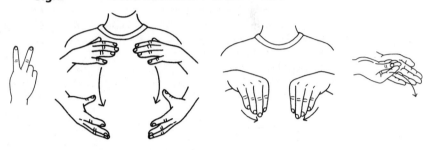

Krista: If I buy blouses, I'll need pants.
Sign: IF BLOUSES BUY — PANTS NEED ME

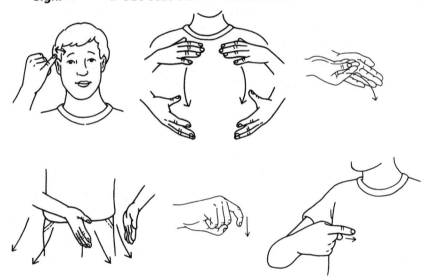

Robert: Use your credit card.
Sign: CREDIT (outline card) — YOURS USE

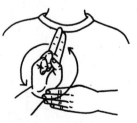

Shopping Superlatives and Comparisons

In English, we sometimes form words that compare by adding endings, such as "est" or "er." In Sign, comparatives and superlatives aren't used. You just use the root (base) word. For example, **greatest** is signed simply as **great,** and **happier** is signed **happy.** However, you can compare objects another way, using Sign. After you decide which base word you want to use, sign it and then add one of the following words from Table 6-10 — whichever one is the most appropriate.

Comparing costs is a pretty common thing to do. Here's how to sign the better bargain. If you're at the store, you can always point to what you're referring to; this way you can avoid fingerspelling. To sign that you found the cheapest or most expensive item, simply sign **cheap** or **expensive** and then sign the word **top.** This is a good way to compare several prices. You can also sign cheap or expensive and then sign **better.**

Table 6-10		Super Words		
English	*Sign*		*English*	*Sign*
GOOD			BETTER	
BEST			TOP	

(continued)

Table 6-10 (continued)

English	Sign	English	Sign
BOTTOM		BAD	
WORSE/ WORST			

English: The red shirt is better than the green.
Sign: RED SHIRT — GREEN SHIRT — RED (point) BETTER

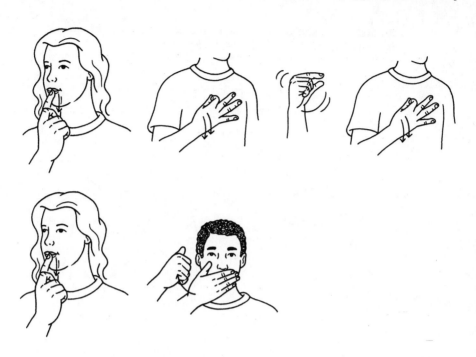

English: His coat is the warmest.
Sign: HIS COAT — WARM — TOP

English: Your shoes are the ugliest.
Sign: YOUR SHOES — UGLY — WORST

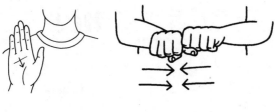

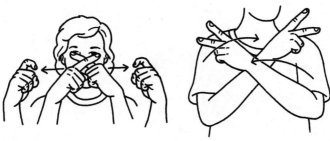

Fun & Games

Match the Signs with their corresponding words by drawing a line between each pair. You can find the answers in Appendix A.

1.

a. Blue _____

b. Umbrella _____

c. Money _____

2.
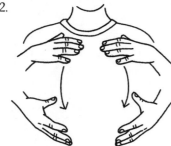

d. Pants _____

e. Purse _____

f. Check _____

3.

g. Yellow _____

h. Blouse _____

4.

5.
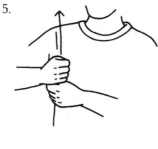

(continued)

6.

7.

8.

Chapter 7

The Signer About Town

- -

In This Chapter

▶ Going out on the town

▶ Signing days and weeks

- -

Going about town, you see Deaf people signing at every turn. Because you're reading this book and discovering ways to communicate in Sign, stopping to chat with them is no longer difficult.

The Signs in this chapter give you an edge on conversing with other Signers about the world of culture and entertainment. After you familiarize yourself with this chapter, you can discuss movies, plays, the theater, and even exhibits in a museum.

And because you can't make a date to see a show if you don't know how to indicate the day and time you're meeting, we include a section that covers those subjects as well.

Making Plans

Getting together with friends to take on the town has never been so easy. The Signs in Table 7-1 can help get you on your way.

 Some timely tips to pencil in: **Appointment** and **reservation** are the same Sign, so if you can sign one, you've got the other. **Schedule** looks like the grid on a calendar page. **Socialize** is one thumb circling the other. **Write down** and **record** share the same Sign. To **cancel an appointment or date** is exactly as it seems — make an **X** on your passive hand.

Table 7-1		Planning Signs	
English	*Sign*	*English*	*Sign*
APPOINTMENT/ RESERVATION		CALENDAR	
CANCEL		DATE	
EVENT		SCHEDULE	
SOCIALIZE		WRITE DOWN	

The following sentences are sure to help you make or break plans:

English: Write it down on your calendar.
Sign: YOUR CALENDAR — WRITE DOWN

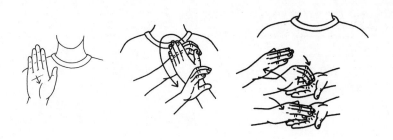

English: We have reservations.
Sign: RESERVATIONS — HAVE US

English: What is your schedule for tomorrow?
Sign: TOMORROW — YOUR SCHEDULE — WHAT Q

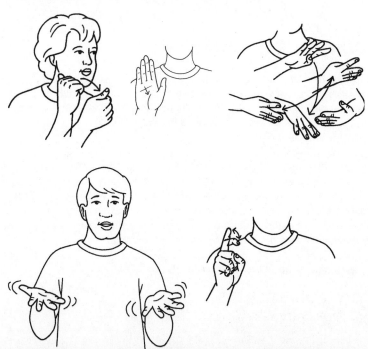

English: The event was cancelled.
Sign: FINISH — EVENT — CANCEL

Finish is signed to show the sentence is past tense. See Chapter 2.

When you need to sign what time something occurs, or if you're giving the time, all you do is touch your wrist where you normally wear your watch and then sign the number. For example, if you want to tell someone that it's 2:00, touch your wrist and then sign the number 2. To distinguish between a.m. and p.m., you sign **morning, afternoon,** or **night** after the number. An exception to that rule: For **midnight,** you simply sign the number 12 straight down; don't touch your wrist. You sign **12 noon** straight up.

Check out the Signs for numbers on the Cheat Sheet at the front of this book. You can then make a date for a specific day and time with the cute Deaf guy or girl you just met. The "Talking About Time" section later in this chapter gives you Signs for relative times, such as **today** and **tomorrow.**

Going to the movies

Sitting around the house and watching a good TV program can be done with your Deaf friends if your TV has closed captioning (CC), which allows the text to appear on the screen. If the captioning doesn't come on, just give it a minute. Videotapes work the same way. Many Deaf people rent videotapes to see captioned movies.

Open captioning (OC) is different. This captioning is the subtitles you usually see on foreign films. In case you were wondering, yes, Deaf people attend movies. Many Deaf people attend the movies to see the latest flicks and go to dinner afterward. Some theaters usually have an OC Night on newly released movies. This is a good place to meet Deaf people. Call your local theater to see whether it has a captioning night for the Deaf.

To sign **open captioning,** simply fingerspell O-C.

CULTURAL WISDOM

Communicating during a movie is common among Signers. They converse about everything — the movie plot, an actor, even the lack of salt on the popcorn. Table 7-2 presents some Signs to help you enjoy the show.

Table 7-2	Movie and TV Terms		
English	*Sign*	*English*	*Sign*
ACTING/ACTOR/ ACTRESS/ DRAMA/STAR		CLOSED- CAPTIONED	
MATINEE		MOVIE	
SOLD OUT		TICKETS	

Are you feeling a bit like Bond, James Bond, or are you more in the mood for bonding in a romantic way? Table 7-3 shows you Signs that indicate various types of movies.

Table 7-3	Movie Genres		
English	*Sign*	*English*	*Sign*
ACTION		COMEDY/ FUNNY	
MYSTERY		ROMANCE	
FANTASY			

English: The movie sold out.
Sign: MOVIE — SOLD OUT

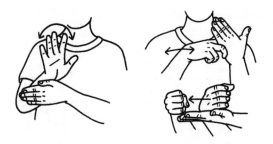

English: If the movie is open-captioned, I'll go.
Sign: IF MOVIE O-C — ME GO

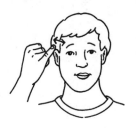 

 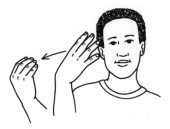

English: The matinee was a comedy.
Sign: AFTERNOON MOVIE — FUNNY

English: We went to see the new mystery.
Sign: FINISH — NEW MYSTERY — SEE US

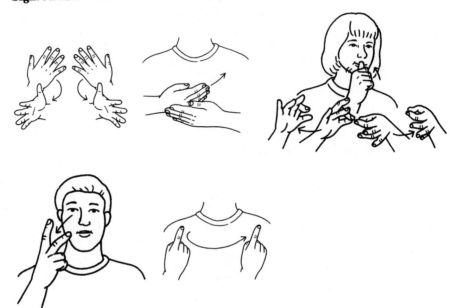

Mystery is signed the same way as the word strange, so a good mystery is strange.

English: There's captioning Saturday at the movie.
Sign: SATURDAY MOVIE — O-C

Going to the theater

Attending plays is always a great way to improve your Signing skills — especially if the actors also sign. Many live-performance plays provide an interpreter, so Deaf people are able to attend and enjoy plays along with hearing folks.

In this section, we show you a few of the more well-known theatrical terms that you may want to know, starting with the ones in Table 7-4.

Table 7-4		Theatrical Terms	
English	*Sign*	*English*	*Sign*
INTERMISSION		LIGHTS	
THEATER		STAGE	

Light bulb is signed with a **flick,** using your index finger and thumb under your chin, and then mimicking the action of screwing in or taking out a light bulb. You can sign light and mimic as to shining a spotlight or a flashlight. **Stage** doesn't allow the passive hand to move, only the active one outward.

English: When the lights go out, stop talking.
Sign: LIGHTS OUT — TALKING STOP

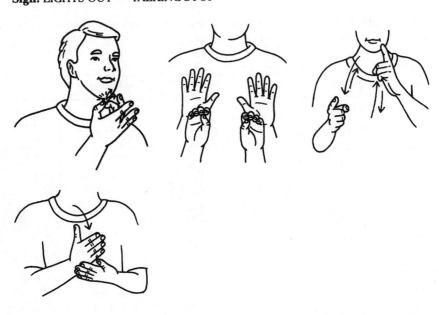

English: During intermission, I'm leaving.
Sign: DURING INTERMISSION — LEAVE ME

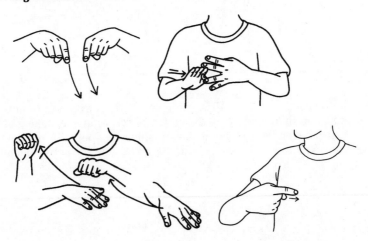

Going to the museum

Visiting a museum is quite an experience, and one that many Deaf people can appreciate as easily as the hearing world. You don't have to be able to hear to enjoy all the wonderful things that are included in museums. However, being able to discuss what you see is nice.

Use the Signs in Table 7-5 when you go back in time for a few hours.

Table 7-5		Museums	
English	*Sign*	*English*	*Sign*
ART		DISPLAY/ EXHIBIT/ SHOW	
HISTORY		MUSEUM	
TIME/ERA			

Museum is signed like house only you use the manual **M** on both hands. Signing about time periods is done by signing the manual **T** in a circular motion with your active hand on your passive hand. This means **time** or **era**.

Table 7-6 shows how to describe some of the things you might see inside a museum.

Table 7-6	Museum Displays		
English	*Sign*	*English*	*Sign*
PAINT/ PAINTING		PHOTOGRAPHY	
SCULPT/ SCULPTURE			

Here are some Signs that have similar hand shapes and meanings. **Photograph** and **picture** are signed the same; add **painting** to this when it's used as a noun. **Photography** is signed by mimicking taking a picture. Make sure that you give it a double click because a single click means to take a picture. **Paint** is signed with the active hand, **painting** with the passive hand (use four fingers). **Sculpture** and **sculpt** are very similar: Sign **sculpture** with the manual **A** on both hands — twist them while simultaneously going downward. **Sculpt** is made with an **A** handshape also. Mimic as if you're putting your thumbs in it and making something while going downward.

English: The museum is open.
Sign: MUSEUM — OPEN

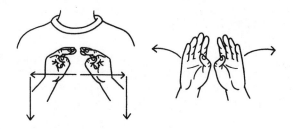

English: The picture is old.
Sign: PICTURE — OLD

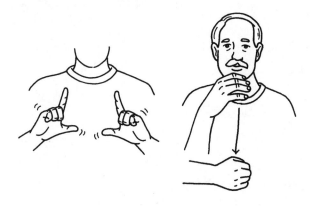

English: We saw the photography exhibit.
Sign: FINISH — PHOTOGRAPHY EXHIBIT SEE

Talking About Time

Half the fun of going to movies, plays, and museums lies in setting up a date and anticipating the treat. This section helps you make your plans by showing you how to sign not only what time you want to go but also which day or even which week. Check out Table 7-7 for the days of the week.

Table 7-7		Days of the Week	
English	*Sign*	*English*	*Sign*
MONDAY		TUESDAY	
WEDNESDAY		THURSDAY	
FRIDAY		SATURDAY	
SUNDAY			

Use the first letter in the manual alphabet to sign the **weekdays** and **Saturday,** but use **T-H** for **Thursday. Sunday** is signed in a circular motion.

If you want to make plans for the weekend, you need to know how to sign **weekend.** Table 7-8 shows you that sign and more.

Table 7-8		Time-Sensitive Signs	
English	**Sign**	**English**	**Sign**
DAY		WEEK	
WEEKEND		MONTH	
YEAR		TODAY	
TOMORROW		YESTERDAY	

(continued)

Table 7-8 (continued)

English	Sign	English	Sign
LAST YEAR		NEXT WEEK	

Signin' the Sign

Denni and Wanda want to go to the movies, so they decide to schedule a time that works for the both of them.

Denni: Want to go to a movie?
Sign: MOVIE — GO WANT Q

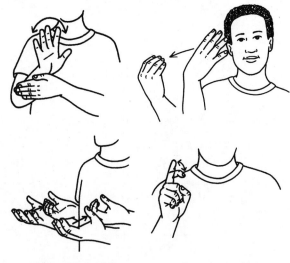

Wanda: Yes, I can go next Saturday — maybe a comedy.
Sign: YES — NEXT WEEK — SATURDAY — GO FUNNY
               MOVIE — MAYBE

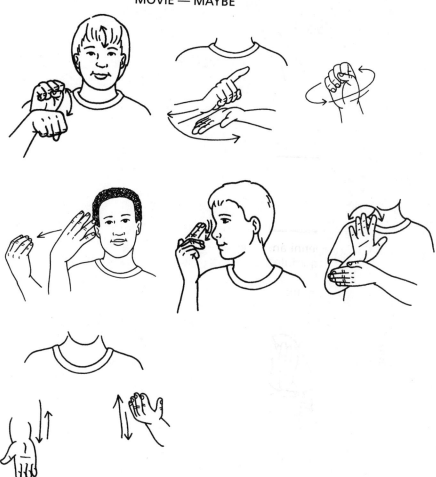

Denni: I'll write it down on my schedule.
Sign: SCHEDULE — WRITE DOWN — ME WILL

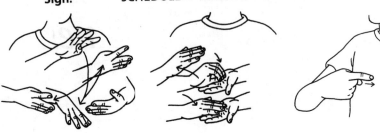

Wanda: I'll write it down, too.
Sign: WRITE DOWN — TOO — ME WILL

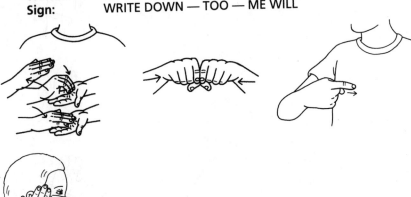

Fun & Games

Match the days of the week with their corresponding Signs. You can find the answers in Appendix A.

1. Sunday

a.

2. Monday

b.

3. Tuesday

c.

4. Wednesday

d.

5. Thursday

e.

(continued)

6. Friday

f.

7. Saturday

g.

Chapter 8

Enjoying Yourself Come Rain or Shine

You can relax in many ways. This chapter covers a few of the more active pastimes. We provide Signs for sports, recreations, and hobbies in this chapter. And because you probably don't want to have a picnic in the rain, this chapter also deals with Signs for the weather.

Exercising Your Right to Recreate

All work and no play makes Jack a dull boy — or so the saying goes. The point is that everyone loves to get out and play once in a while, whether on a team or individually. This section gives Signs for various team sports first, and then, for those of you who are more independent, Signs for solo sports. Have fun!

Getting into the competitive spirit

The majority of sports Signs look like what they represent. For example, the Signs for **tennis** and **baseball** mimic the swing of a racket and bat, respectively. Don't you just love it when Signing is this easy? Check out the Signs in Table 8-1 for more team sports Signs.

Table 8-1		Competitive Team Sports	
English	*Sign*	*English*	*Sign*
BASEBALL		BASKETBALL	
BOXING		FOOTBALL	
HOCKEY		SOCCER	
WRESTLING		TENNIS	

Signing **ball** is easy: Mimic putting both hands on a ball; do it with a double motion. You can make the ball as small or as big as you want.

Wrestling and football are made the same way: Lock your fingers together; just don't bend your fingers. If you do this with a double motion, that's **football.** Lock your fingers once and go side to side, and you've signed **wrestling.**

Box and **boxing** are the same Sign. Put your fists up as if to be in a boxing stance. No two people hold up their fists the same way, so the Sign varies from person to person.

Table 8-2 gives you Signs for competitive terms. Some of these Signs are a bit tricky, so allow us to give you some explanation.

Match, game, and **challenge** are signed the same. Game and match get a double motion, though, and challenge gets a single motion.

If you want to sign **versus,** use the same Sign as the one for challenge.

Compete, sports, and **race** are all signed the same way. Make the manual A handshape with both hands, put your palms together and then alternate them back and forth. If you want to show fierce competition, grit your teeth and alternate your hands rapidly.

Signing **referee** or **umpire** is as simple as putting both index and middle fingertips on your lips, like blowing a whistle. You'll probably see many Signs for these two words, but this Sign seems to be pretty well used.

Here's a helping tip: **Score** is signed just like **count.**

Tournament starts the Sign with both hands in the same handshape — index and middle fingers bent, palms facing addressee with your dominant hand higher than your passive hand. Now, alternate them up and down like a round robin tournament.

Lose and **lost** are the same Sign. Make the manual V handshape with your dominant hand and then allow it to hit your passive palm.

Table 8-2	Competitive Terms		
English	*Sign*	*English*	*Sign*
MATCH/GAME/ CHALLENGE		CHAMPION/ CHAMPIONSHIP	

(continued)

Table 8-2 *(continued)*

English	Sign	English	Sign
RACE/COMPETE/ SPORTS		REFEREE/ UMPIRE	
SCORE		TEAM	
TOURNAMENT		LOSE/LOST	
WIN/WON			

Here's how to put these Signs into ASL sentences. Replace these sport Signs with other sport Signs; you'll have more ASL sentences packed in your punch.

English: The soccer game was good.
Sign: SOCCER GAME — GOOD

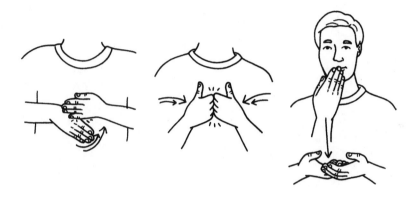

English: He can box and wrestle.
Sign: BOX — WRESTLE — BOTH CAN HIM

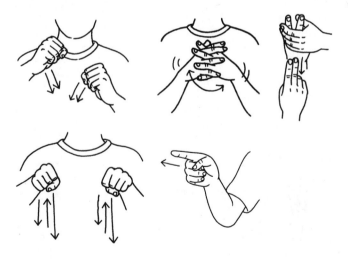

English: If you play soccer, you can't play basketball.
Sign: IF SOCCER PLAY YOU — BASKETBALL PLAY YOU — CAN'T

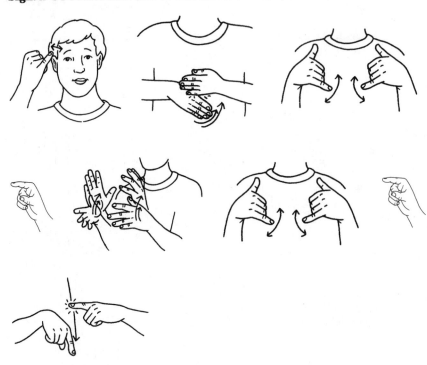

English: Our team won the race.
Sign: OUR TEAM — RACE — WON

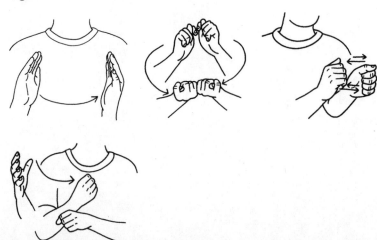

English: He's a football player.
Sign: FOOTBALL — PLAY HIM

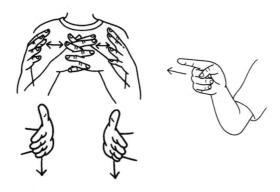

English: What's the score?
Sign: SCORE WHAT Q

English: Did we win or lose?
Sign: WIN — LOSE — US WHICH Q

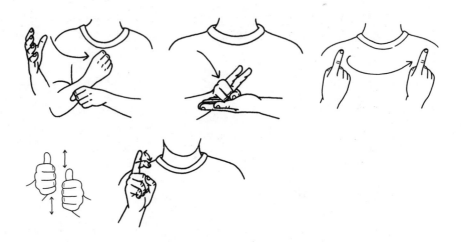

Setting out solo

You don't have to compete with a bunch of other people to be active and enjoy the great outdoors. Table 8-3 gives you the Signs for sports that you can enjoy all by yourself if you want.

Table 8-3	Individual Sports		
English	*Sign*	*English*	*Sign*
CYCLING		GOLF	
HIKING		JOGGING	

English	Sign	English	Sign
SWIMMING		RUNNING	
WALKING			

When you sign **jog,** make your fists in the "S" handshapes, put them beside your body, and move them as though you're jogging while alternating your arms. You sign **race** by making both hands in the "A" handshapes. Bring them together with both thumbs facing up, then alternate the thumbs back and forth like two people racing. This is why this Sign also means **compete** and **sport.**

The following Signs aren't really sports but are fun to do outside nonetheless:

PICNIC

CAMPING

The following sentences show sports Signs in action.

Glide your hands down the sides of your body after signing a sport to change the sport to the player: golf to golfer, run to runner, and so on.

English: Mark is a good golfer.
Sign: M-A-R-K — GOOD GOLF (AGENT)

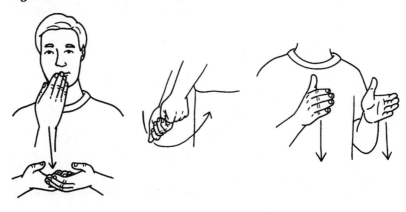

English: Do you like cycling?
Sign: CYCLING — YOU LIKE Q

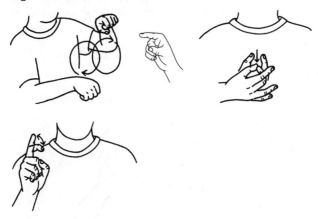

English: Let's go hiking.
Sign: HIKING — US GO

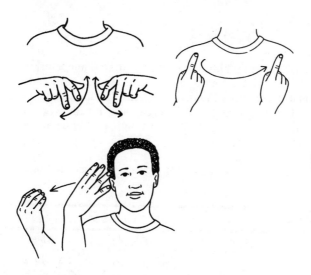

English: We're going on a picnic. Are you coming?
Sign: PICNIC GO US — COME YOU Q

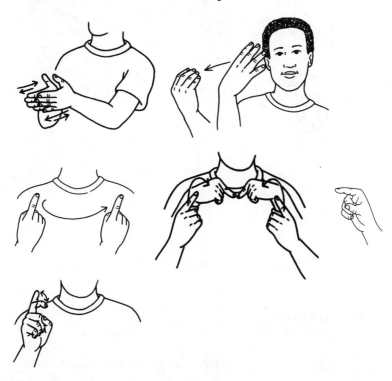

Playing Indoor Games

Not all games are played outside. Nor do all of them have Signs. For example, you fingerspell **cards, video, chess,** and **checkers.** All board and card games are fingerspelled. Mimic throwing dice for **gambling** and dealing cards for any **card games.** After you do this, fingerspell specifically what game you mean. Some indoor games do have Signs, though, and you can find many of them in Table 8-4 — no cheating!

If your Deaf friends have a local Sign for a game, just use that Sign instead.

Table 8-4	Indoor Games		
English	*Sign*	*English*	*Sign*
BETTING		BOARD GAME	
DEAL CARDS		GAMBLING	
VIDEO GAMES			

English: Who wants to play poker?
Sign: P-O-K-E-R — WANTS — WHO Q

English: Deal the cards.
Sign: DEAL CARDS

English: He likes playing chess.
Sign: C-H-E-S-S — HE LIKES

English: Do you gamble?
Sign: GAMBLE YOU Q

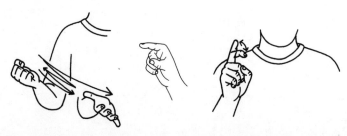

Having Fun with Hobbies

From collecting to surfing the Web, hobbies keep you busy and entertained and, sometimes, even educated. The signs in Table 8-5 show you how to tell people about your hobby and make it come alive!

Table 8-5		Hobbies	
English	*Sign*	*English*	*Sign*
COLLECTING		BROWSING THE INTERNET	
KNITTING		READING	

English	Sign	English	Sign
SEWING		STAMP COLLECTING	

You sign **browsing the Internet** by showing the Sign for **Internet,** then sign **read. Stamp collecting** is **stamp** then **collect** — like gathering a bunch of stamps into the palm of your hand.

English: I collect stamps.
Sign: STAMPS — COLLECT ME

English: Knitting is relaxing.
Sign: KNITTING — RELAXING

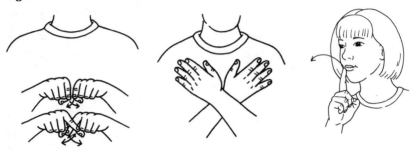

English: I like sewing.
Sign: SEWING — LIKE ME

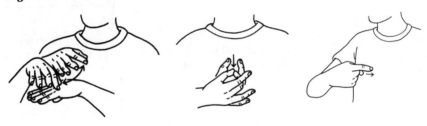

Getting the Weather Report

When isn't the weather a popular topic for discussion? Practice the Signs in Table 8-6, and you'll be as right as rain.

Table 8-6	Weather Wise		
English	**Sign**	**English**	**Sign**
CLOUDY		DARK	

English	Sign	English	Sign
THUNDER		LIGHTNING	
STORM		SUNNY	
WINDY		OUTSIDE	
WEATHER			

Check out these weather Signs and give them a whirl. Try replacing them with other weather Signs — it'll be smooth sailing.

English: It is cloudy today.
Sign: TODAY — CLOUDY

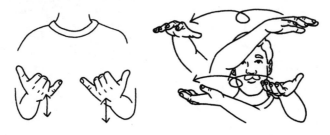

English: It's sunny outside.
Sign: OUTSIDE SUNNY

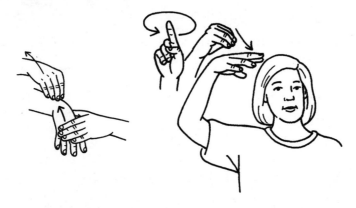

English: It's dark and windy this evening.
Sign: NOW NIGHT — DARK WINDY

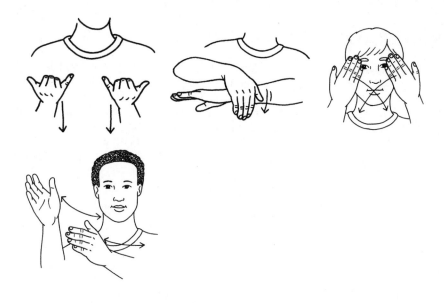

English: There is thunder and lightning outside.
Sign: OUTSIDE — THUNDER LIGHTNING

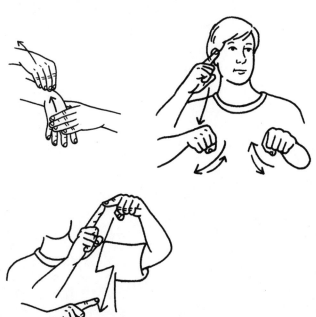

Asking Rhetorical Questions

Asking a rhetorical question is a one-person show. You don't really want a response, although your eyebrows are raised at the who, what, why, where question Signs and go down when you answer. You want to ask and answer the question yourself. A rhetorical question is a way of making a point and giving information. Keep your eyebrows up when you ask the question — that action tells everyone that you don't expect an answer. You will know these are rhetorical questions when the Signer gives no pause before answering his own question. The hands never go down to give you a chance to put your hands up to respond.

English: Brent is on my team.
Sign: MY TEAM WHO — B-R-E-N-T

English: The tournament is in Pueblo.
Sign: TOURNAMENT WHERE — P-U-E-B-L-O

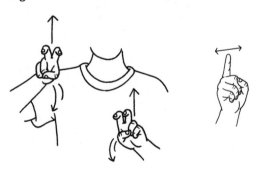

Signin' the Sign

Jason and Jesse can't decide what they want to do tomorrow — it just depends on the weather.

Jesse: I want to go golf tomorrow.
Sign: TOMORROW — GOLF — GO WANT ME

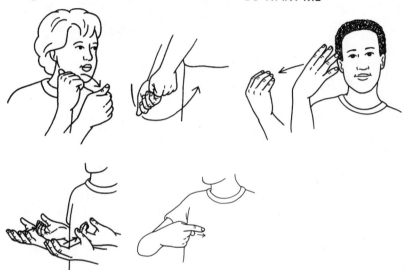

Jason: I'll go swimming tomorrow.
Sign: TOMORROW — SWIM ME

Jesse: If it rains, are you going swimming?
Sign: IF RAIN — YOU SWIMMING Q

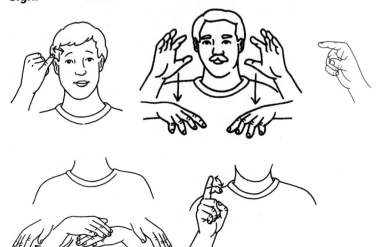

Jason: No, I'll stay home and read.
Sign: NO — HOME STAY — READ

Jesse: If it rains, let's play cards.
Sign: IF RAIN — CARDS US

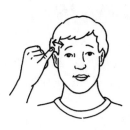

Fun & Games

Fill in the blanks with a sign. Go to Appendix A (or look through this chapter) to find out what the Signs are.

1. Let's go to the park and have a _____. We'll invite the ants, too!

2. It is _____ outside. Did you bring a flashlight?

3. You need to _____. You seem stressed.

4. No _____ allowed. We're just playing for fun.

5. Do you play _____? I brought my bat and glove just in case.

6. The _____ is over; we won.

7. I don't like _____ and lightning during storms.

8. I went to a _____ match. Those guys are really strong!

a.

b.

c.

d.

e.

f.

g.

h.

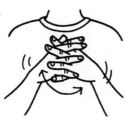

Chapter 9

Home and Office

. . . .

. . . .

*Y*ou can set up shop at home or in a traditional office. This chapter tells you how to sign rooms and furnishings for both places. The final touch will be seeing how it all fits together.

Discussing Your Office

Many more Deaf people are working in office situations than ever before, so there's never been a better time to know Signs around the office. Use these Signs if you want to show Deaf visitors around the office or if you have a Deaf colleague at your place of work.

Occupying yourself with occupations

The average American worker changes occupations many times in the course of a career. Table 9-1 gives you Signs for some of the occupations you may want to try at some point.

Table 9-1		Occupations	
English	**Sign**	**English**	**Sign**
ASSISTANT		BOSS	
WORKER/ EMPLOYEE		DIRECTOR/ MANAGER	
SECRETARY		SUPERVISOR	

Here are some sentences that will surely come in handy at the office.

English: When is payday?
Sign: PAYDAY — WHEN Q

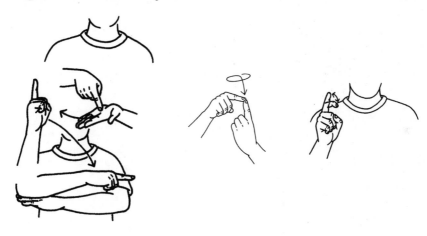

English: She was terminated by Human Resources.
Sign: H-R TERMINATE HER

Most people refer to Human Resources as "HR," so this term is signed by fingerspelling H-R.

English: The boss has my time sheet.
Sign: TIME SHEET MINE — BOSS HAVE

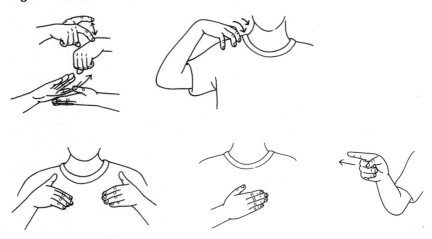

Spying office supplies

Moving around the cubicle, you have many things to sign. Try the Signs in Table 9-2, and you'll be the boss.

You may find the Sign for **clock** to be a bit tricky, but it's really pretty simple. Touch your wrist where your watch is worn and then make both hands into manual C handshapes toward the wall.

Table 9-2		Office Equipment	
English	*Sign*	*English*	*Sign*
CLOCK		OFFICE	

English	Sign	English	Sign
PAPER		COPY MACHINE	
PAPER CLIP		DESK/ TABLE	
PENCIL		EQUIPMENT	

(continued)

Table 9-2 (continued)

English	Sign	English	Sign
PHONE		LAPTOP	
STAPLER			

The office is a great place to work these Signs. The following sentences can give you a hand with some office items. And because office equipment doesn't always work, Signs exist for that, too.

English: The fax machine is busy.
Sign: F-A-X MACHINE — BUSY

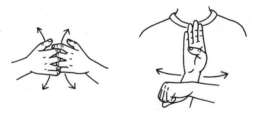

English: The copy machine is broken.
Sign: COPY MACHINE — BROKE

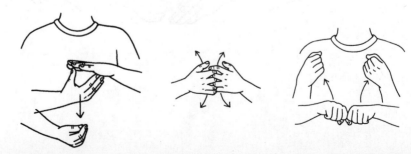

GRAMMATICALLY SPEAKING

Sign **broke** or **broken** like you're breaking a stick with both hands in the manual S handshape.

English: My computer is frozen.
Sign: MY COMPUTER — FROZE

 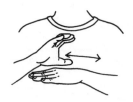 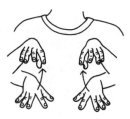

 GRAMMATICALLY SPEAKING

Sign **froze** or **frozen** like the word freeze (see Chapter 5).

English: Where is the stapler?
Sign: STAPLER WHERE Q

English: Do we have enough paper?
Sign: PAPER ENOUGH HAVE Q

 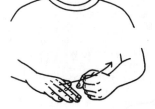 

Getting to work

The workday world is full of tasks from stocking shelves to attending meetings. The Signs in Table 9-3 make work a little more fun — you can carry on a private conversation with another Signer during a boring meeting.

Table 9-3		Business Terms	
English	*Sign*	*English*	*Sign*
BUSINESS		CLOSED DOWN	
DISCUSS		MEETING/ CONFERENCE	
PROMOTION		STOCKS	

English	Sign	English	Sign
TRADE (stocks)		WORK	

Put these work-related Signs into action in the following:

English: Are you going to the conference?
Sign: CONFERENCE GO YOU Q

English: The manager's meeting is upstairs.
Sign: MANAGERS MEETING — UPSTAIRS

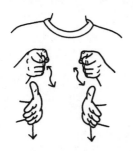

English: If you trade stocks, I will, too.
Sign: IF TRADE STOCKS YOU — ME SAME

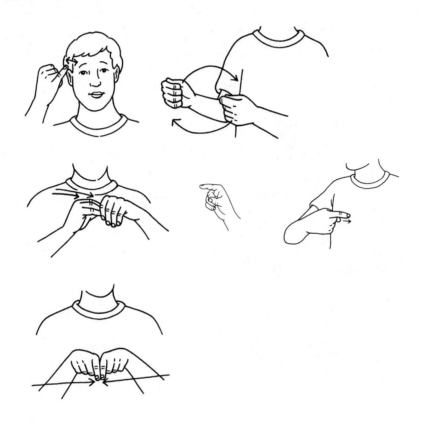

English: Where do you work?
Sign: WORK YOU WHERE Q

English: The business is closed.
Sign: BUSINESS CLOSED

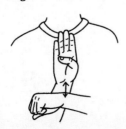 

Handling Signs about Your Home

You can give the grand tour without one word of explanation. Notice how the
Signs in Table 9-4 let your fingers do the talking.

Table 9-4		Dwelling Signs	
English	**Sign**	**English**	**Sign**
DOOR		FLOOR	
GARAGE		HOME	
HOUSE		LIVE	

(continued)

Table 9-4 (continued)

English	Sign	English	Sign
LOCK		OWN	
RENT		WINDOW	
YARD		UPSTAIRS	
DOWNSTAIRS			

To sign **condo,** you fingerspell C-O-N-D-O, and to sign **apartment,** you use the abbreviation and fingerspell just A-P-T.

English: Do you own your home or rent?
Sign: YOUR HOME — OWN — RENT WHICH Q

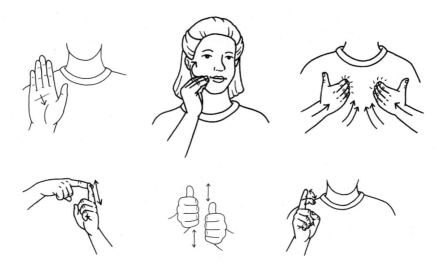

English: The door is locked.
Sign: DOOR — LOCKED

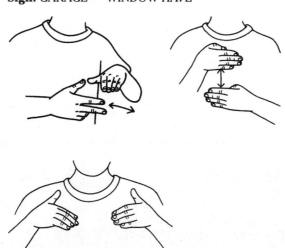

English: The garage has a window.
Sign: GARAGE — WINDOW HAVE

English: His house is big.
Sign: HIS HOUSE — BIG

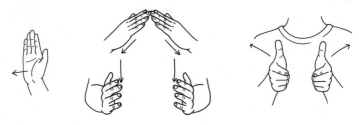

English: Can I go upstairs?
Sign: UPSTAIRS — GO ME CAN Q

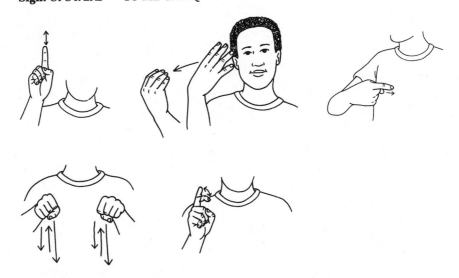

Touring all the rooms

Touring the house room by room has many surprises. One surprise is that each room has its own Sign. (Well, maybe that's not so surprising.) Table 9-5 gives most of them.

The Sign for **closet** has several motions, so here's some explanation: With your dominant hand, make a hook with your index finger. This finger acts as a hanger. Your passive index finger acts as a pole on which to put the hangers. Put several "hangers" onto the "pole."

Table 9-5		Rooms	
English	*Sign*	*English*	*Sign*
BASEMENT		BATHROOM	
BEDROOM		CLOSET	
DINING ROOM		KITCHEN	
LIVING ROOM			

English: Can I use the bathroom?
Sign: BATHROOM — USE ME CAN Q

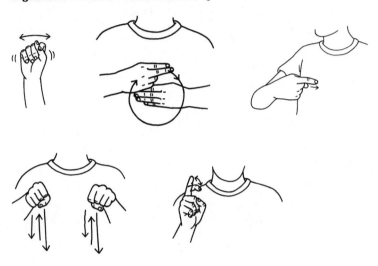

English: Is this your bedroom?
Sign: BEDROOM — YOURS Q

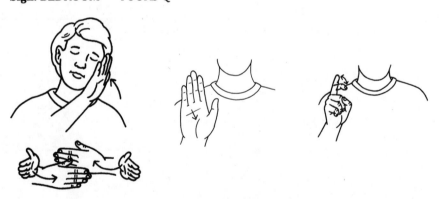

English: The kitchen is hot.
Sign: KITCHEN — HOT

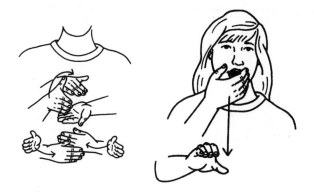

English: Don't play in the living room.
Sign: LIVING ROOM — PLAY THERE — DON'T

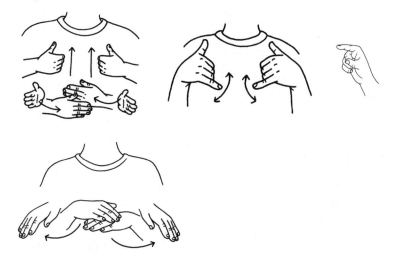

Furnishing your home

After you have rooms, you can start filling them with furniture. Table 9-6 shows you the Signs for everything from window treatments to carpet.

After you have the Sign for **chair** down, you'll have no problem with **love seat** or **couch.** To sign love seat, sign chair (double motion); then, with the same handshape, put your dominant hand next to your passive hand to show a couch for two. To sign couch, make the Sign for chair (single motion); then have your dominant hand go outward to show several seats.

Table 9-6		Home Furnishings	
English	*Sign*	*English*	*Sign*
BED		BLINDS	
CARPET		CHAIR	
COUCH		CURTAINS	
LAMP		LOVE SEAT	

English	Sign	English	Sign
PICTURES		RECLINER	
TABLE		VASE	

If you're comfortable with these furnishings, try the following sentences.

English: Sit on the couch.
Sign: COUCH — SIT

English: Turn on the lamp.
Sign: LAMP O-N

English: My carpet is white.
Sign: MY CARPET — WHITE

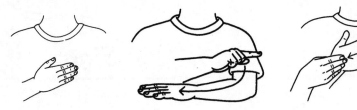

English: The picture is crooked.
Sign: PICTURE — CROOKED

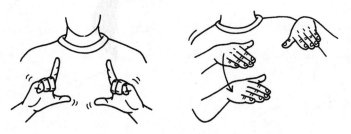

Keeping Track of Your Subjects in Space

At work or at home, you're always talking about people who aren't right there with you. For instance, at work, you may be discussing with one of your co-workers how much you like your boss. When using Sign, you don't have to be able to see someone (or something) to be able to talk about him, her, or it. (It's a good thing, too. How else could you plan a surprise party for your spouse?)

All you have to do to discuss someone who isn't physically present is assign that person a point in the space near your passive hand. You use the same Sign for **he, she,** and **it** — your index finger extended in a pointing gesture (see Chapter 1). If the he, she, or it is nearby, your index finger points at them, but if they're not in your general vicinity, you select a specific place in the space in front of you to sort of "stand in" for the person you're discussing. You point to that same space every time you refer to the absent one. So if you want to sign about Buddy, fingerspell his name and point to your passive hand area.

Signin' the Sign

Dave and Debby have just purchased their first house. Here's what they have to say about it.

Dave: The house has a big yard.
Sign: HOUSE YARD — BIG

Debbie: I want to see the kitchen.
Sign: KITCHEN — WANT SEE ME

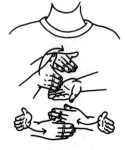 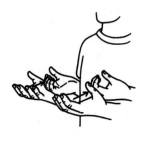 

Dave: We need a couch, lamp, and pictures.
Sign: COUCH LAMP PICTURES — NEED US

 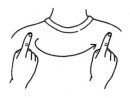

Debbie: It's great to own, not rent, a house.
Sign: HOUSE — OWN GREAT — RENT NOT

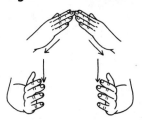 

Fun & Games

Alice is a new supervisor at her job. She's at a meeting explaining what needs to be done tomorrow.

Fill in the gaps in her explanation.

Please use the (a)_____ only on Thursdays. Also, your (b)_____ is broken; it keeps crashing, but we're sending for someone to fix it. Please tell the other (c)_____ not to be late or they will be (d)_____. I will have my (e)_____ with me tomorrow. We will discuss (f)_____ on Monday in my (g)_____. I want to (h)_____ more people.

1.

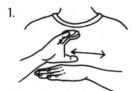

2.

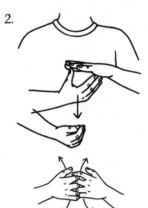

3.

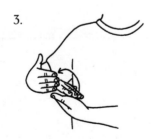

4.

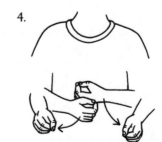

5.

6.

7.

8.

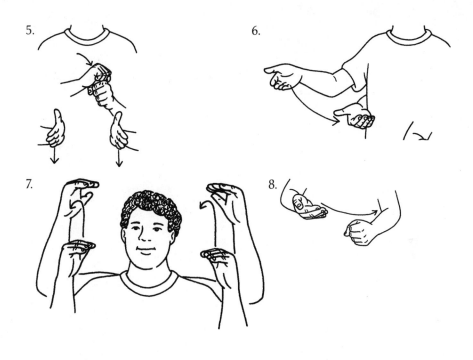

Part III
Signing On the Go

The 5th Wave

By Rich Tennant

"He's still wrestling with the ethical conundrum of a professional mime learning ASL."

In this part . . .

The chapters in this part add direction to your Signing. You find out how to sign landmarks and directions, so that you can tell a Deaf person how to get somewhere or find out how to get to a particular destination yourself. This part also gives you a glimpse of some medical terms and body parts that may be a big help in certain situations, not necessarily just the medical ones.

Chapter 10

Asking Directions and Getting Around

*G*etting where you need to go can happen as quickly as a wave of your hand. You can go a long way by using these Signs for directions and transportation.

Finding Your Way

When giving or getting directions in Sign, you need to keep two things in mind. Get these strategies down, and you can tell people exactly where to go and how to get there:

✔ Try to start with a point of reference that's familiar to both of you, such as a store, restaurant, or bridge, then give the directions.

✔ Go from big to small; from general to specific.

For example, in the States, you go from state to city to neighborhood to street to house number.

Table 10-1 groups Signs for compass points and other directional signals. Notice that the handshapes you use for the **compass points** and for **left** and **right** are the first letters of the words.

Table 10-1		Compass Points	
English	*Sign*	*English*	*Sign*
NORTH		SOUTH	
EAST		WEST	
LEFT		RIGHT	

The following examples show you how to sign directions in perfect order.

English: My house is west of the store.
Sign: STORE — MY HOUSE WEST

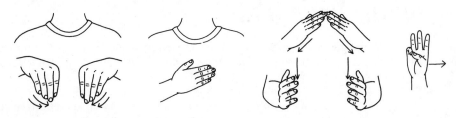

English: Turn right twice.
Sign: RIGHT — RIGHT

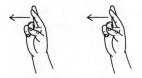

Notice that you don't use once, twice, and so on; you simply sign **right** two times (twice).

To give directions, you often establish relationships — don't worry; you don't have to commit for very long. Table 10-2 lists the Signs for the situational relationships you use to give directions as well as some landmarks and distances that you might use.

To sign straight, use the B manual handshape; rest it on your nose while your index finger touches your forehead and then move it straight out in front of you, bending your wrist.

This Sign is also the Sign for "sober" — the sentence's context tells you which one. This same B handshape is used to sign the direction to turn onto a street.

Table 10-2		Directional Relationship Signs	
English	*Sign*	*English*	*Sign*
AFTER		BACK	
BEFORE		BEHIND	
BESIDE		CROSS STREET/ INTERSECTION	

(continued)

Table 10-2 *(continued)*

English	Sign	English	Sign
FORWARD		IN FRONT OF	
STRAIGHT		TURN	

The following sentences put these Signs in action.

English: Go straight; don't turn.
Sign: STRAIGHT — TURN — DON'T

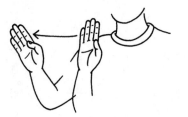  

English: The cross-street is Maple Drive.
Sign: CROSS STREET WHAT — M-A-P-L-E D-R

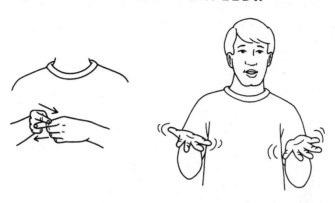

Signin' the Sign

 Buddy is going to the mall. Although he knows Pueblo, he isn't sure how to get to the mall from where he's located. He sees Linda — she knows the town well. Notice how she helps him while using a familiar reference point.

Buddy: How do I get to the mall?
Sign: M-A-L-L ARRIVE — HOW Q

Linda: Do you know where the museum is?
Sign: MUSEUM WHERE — KNOW YOU Q

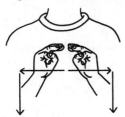 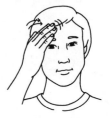

Buddy: From this cross-street I go north.
Sign: HERE CROSS STREET — NORTH GO ME

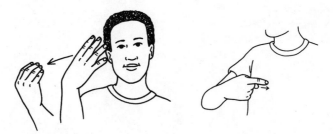

Linda: Yes, but turn east after two miles.
Sign: YES — BUT TWO M-I-L-E-S FINISH — GO EAST

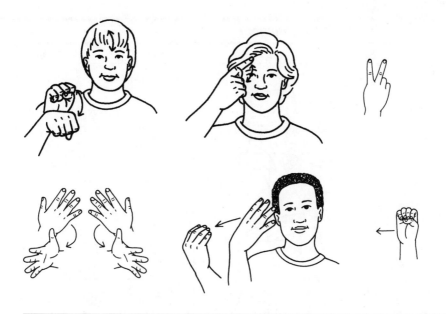

Looking to Natural Landmarks

Most people find landmarks to be helpful when giving or receiving directions. After all, telling someone to turn right at the bottom of the hill is much easier than telling someone to turn right after traveling 1.3 miles. The Signs for natural landmarks in Table 10-3 are sure to help you.

Table 10-3		Natural Landmarks	
English	*Sign*	*English*	*Sign*
FIELD		HILL	

(continued)

Table 10-3 *(continued)*

English	Sign	English	Sign
LAKE		MOUNTAIN	
RIVER		TREE	
WATERFALL			

Take a look at the following sentences to see how you can use these landmark Signs when giving directions.

English: My house is at the top of the big hill.
Sign: BIG HILL — MY HOUSE — TOP

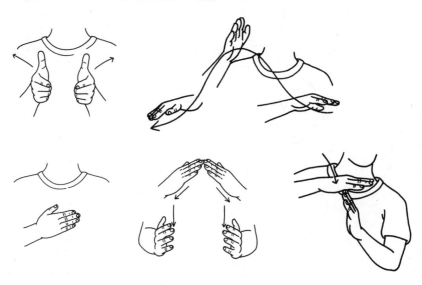

English: Turn left after the field.
Sign: FIELD — LEFT

English: When you get to the lake, turn right.
Sign: LAKE ARRIVE — RIGHT TURN

 In ASL, **get to** is signed as **arrive.**

English: At the base of the mountain is a small store.
Sign: MOUNTAIN BASE — SMALL STORE — THERE

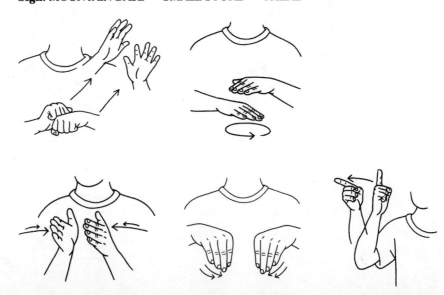

Searching in the City

Going through town can be overwhelming unless you know how to get where you're going. Table 10-4 demonstrates the landmarks you may use to direct someone in the city.

Building is signed with both hands in the H handshape. Place one on top of the other four times; then with B handshapes, palms facing each other, go straight up — go high for a skyscraper.

A **stop sign** is signed by making the Sign for **stop** and then making a square-cut line with your index finger. It would be great to make the octagon shape, but who can?

Table 10-4		Urban Landmarks	
English	*Sign*	*English*	*Sign*
BRIDGE		BUILDING	
GAS STATION		HIGHWAY	

(continued)

Table 10-4 *(continued)*

English	Sign	English	Sign
ROAD/ STREET		STOPLIGHT	
STOP SIGN			

You've no doubt given directions similar to the ones in the following examples. Now, see how to do it in Sign.

English: Pass the park and go three miles south.
Sign: P-A-R-K PASS — SOUTH THREE M-I-L-E-S GO

   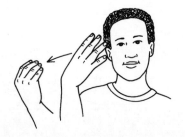

English: At the stop sign, go right.
Sign: STOP SIGN ARRIVE — RIGHT

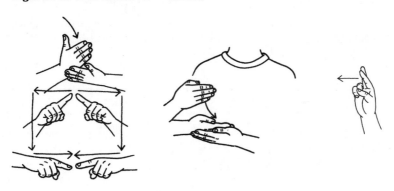

English: Go across the bridge.
Sign: BRIDGE — GO OVER

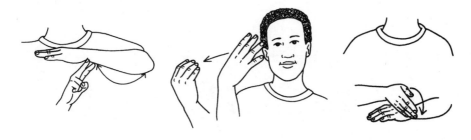

English: The gas station is near the highway.
Sign: HIGHWAY — GAS STATION — NEAR

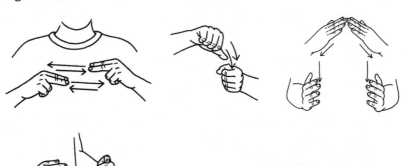

Trotting Out Signs for Transportation

Whether you just need to get around town or decide to see the world, your travel requires wheels. This section gives you just that. Consider the Signs in Table 10-5 for your free-wheeling adventures.

Table 10-5		Wheels	
English	*Sign*	*English*	*Sign*
BICYCLE		CAR	
MOTORCYCLE		PLANE	
SUBWAY		TRAIN	

Bus is fingerspelled B-S — leave out the "u." To sign **driving a bus,** mimic a truck-size steering wheel at the lower chest level, wrap your hands around the imaginary wheel and steer back and forth. This motion also works for trucks, RVs (after you fingerspell R-V), or any large vehicle. Just fingerspell the big rig first.

Get the wheels in motion, so to speak, by using these automotive Signs.

English: The car was in an accident.
Sign: CAR ACCIDENT

Accident is signed by making a 5 handshape, palms facing you, fingertips facing each other. Crash them together, ending in an S handshape.

English: If I miss the train, I'll fly.
Sign: TRAIN MISS — FLY ME

English: You need a motorcycle helmet.
Sign: MOTORCYCLE HELMET — NEED YOU

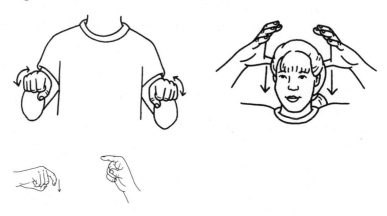

Directing Your Sentences with Conjunctions

As you probably remember from grammar classes of long ago, conjunctions join thoughts or phrases. One of the most common conjunctions is *but,* so let us explain this one first.

In English, *but* has two different meanings. One is used as a conjunction, the other as a preposition. Sometimes, you use *but* to set a condition, as in, "You can go to the party, but you have to be home at midnight." Other times, *but* shows an exception, as in, "Everyone can go but you." The same is true in ASL.

To sign **but** as a conjunction (meaning that a condition is involved), put your dominant hand on the dominant side of your head and flick your index finger twice, ending with your index finger up.

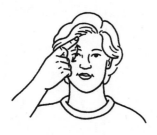

To sign **but** as a preposition (meaning *except*), cross your index fingers to make an "x" and then pull them apart, ending with your two fingers extended.

The following examples show you both situations.

English: Go to the party, but be home at midnight.
Sign: PARTY GO — BUT HOME MIDNIGHT — MUST YOU

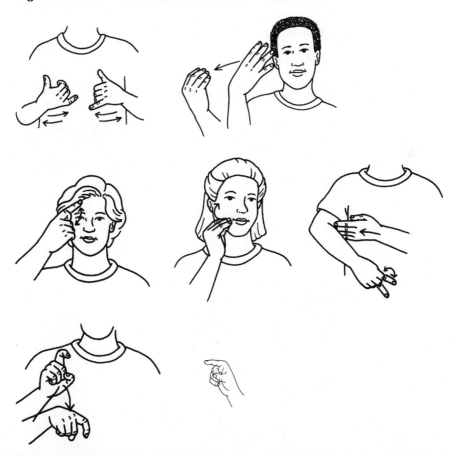

English: Everyone can go but you.
Sign: ALL GO CAN — BUT YOU NOT

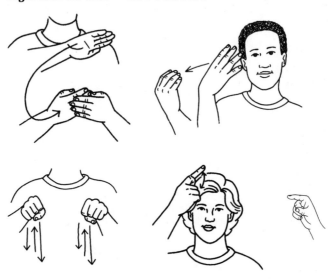

The either/or and neither/nor conjunctions are called *correlative conjunctions,* and you use your hands and head to convey these signs.

When signing **either** . . . **or** and **neither** . . . **nor,** keep in mind that you use these conjunctions to answer questions, not to ask them. So, although you don't use the facial expressions you use to ask questions, you can keep your head still or nod it "yes" for affirmation when you sign either, and you shake your head from side to side while signing neither.

English: Do you want apples or oranges?
Sign: APPLES ORANGES — WANT YOU — WHICH

English response: Either apples or oranges would be fine.
Sign response: EITHER FINE

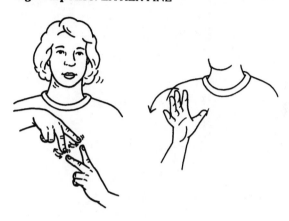

English: Do you want chicken or steak?
Sign: CHICKEN STEAK — WANT YOU — WHICH

English response: I want neither chicken nor steak.
Sign Response: NEITHER

Turn these signed sentences into English.

1. **Sign:**

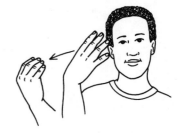

   English:

2. **Sign:**

   English:

3. **Sign:**

 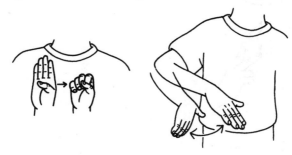

   English:

4. **Sign:**

   English:

(continued)

5. **Sign:**

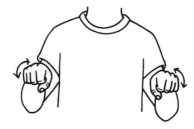 

   English:

6. **Sign:**

   English:

7. **Sign:**

  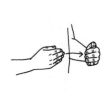

   English:

8. **Sign:**

   English:

9. **Sign:**

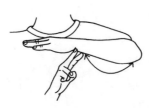  

   English:

10. **Sign:**

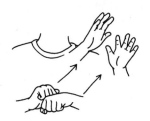

English:

• •

Chapter 11

Here's to Your Health

*T*he medical field has many Signs, and practicing them is fun. However, health and medicine are serious issues. Knowing the following medical Signs doesn't automatically make you a medical interpreter, but you can go a long way in helping someone with regards to illness, the body, and emergencies. In this chapter, we cover some of the main medical-related Signs.

Going to the Doctor

Doctor visits ensure good health. The following sections give you the Signs for the people you deal with and how to tell them your symptoms. These Signs are more helpful than an apple a day — try them and see.

Signaling medical personnel

The doctor is in! Table 11-1 shows the Signs for various medical people.

Table 11-1		Medical Personnel	
English	_Sign_	_English_	_Sign_
CHIROPRACTOR		DENTIST	
DOCTOR		NURSE	
SPECIALIST		SURGEON	

The following sentences are sure to come in handy.

English: The doctor is in.
Sign: DOCTOR HERE

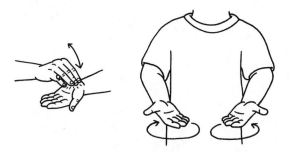

English: You need to see a chiropractor.
Sign: CHIROPRACTOR — GO — NEED YOU

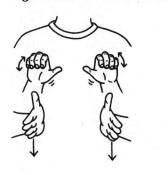
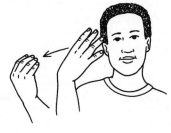

English: Do you need a nurse?
Sign: NURSE — NEED YOU Q

English: The surgeon is a specialist.
Sign: SURGEON SPECIALIST

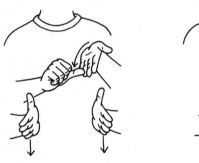 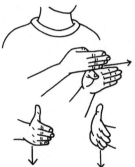

Figuring out how you feel

Knowing the Signs for symptoms of illness can really help you figure out the best way to handle a medical problem. As with talking, signing is sometimes difficult when you don't feel well, but it's a necessary part of receiving help. The Signs in Table 11-2 can take the sting out of communicating your problem.

Table 11-2		Feelings/Symptoms	
English	*Sign*	*English*	*Sign*
COLD		CONSCIOUS	
DIZZY		EARACHE	

English	Sign	English	Sign
HEADACHE		NAUSEA	
UNCONSCIOUS		TEMPERATURE/ FEVER	

Conscious is signed the same way as "know" and "familiar."

Knocked out is signed K-O. With the dominant hand, start the K handshape at eye level with the O handshape ending at your mouth. Complete the Sign with closed eyes while bending your head to the side or in front.

Feeling healthy, wealthy, and wise is great, but allow us to talk about the word feel. Sing **feel** by running your middle finger up your stomach and chest and outward. If you put your thumb up after signing feel, it means **feel good.**

FEEL

Expressing medical terms

Medical words are simple in Sign — they usually look like what they mean. For example, **blood pressure** is signed by making a C handshape with your dominant hand and then placing it on your arm muscle. You then mimic working a pump bulb. **Sutures** and **stitches** are signed by mimicking that you are putting a needle in and out of the stitched area. Check out Table 11-3 to see for yourself.

Table 11-3		Medical Procedures	
English	*Sign*	*English*	*Sign*
BANDAGE		BLOOD PRESSURE	
DRAW BLOOD		INJECTION	
SURGERY		SUTURE/ STITCH	
TEST			

Some Signs are similar in appearance. After you adjust to visually reading ASL, you'll be comfortable in determining the context of the sentence.

Try the following sentences for practice.

English: I need to check your blood pressure.
Sign: YOUR BLOOD PRESSURE — CHECK — ME MUST

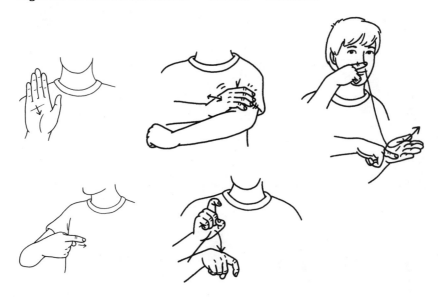

 In ASL, "I" and "me" are signed the same. Just point to yourself with your index finger.

English: He needs an injection.
Sign: INJECTION — NEED HIM

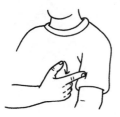

English: How do I get blood drawn?
Sign: ME — BLOOD DRAWN — HOW Q

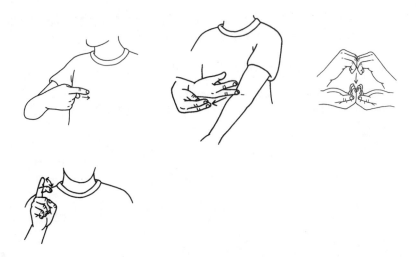

 You fingerspell some medical terms, especially those that are abbreviations anyway. For example, you use the manual alphabet to sign **CPR, ER, OR, MRI, ICU, IV,** and **x-ray,** as well as the names of medications.

Describing Ailments and Treatments

These ailments in Table 11-4 are Signs that many ASL users run into — that explains the bruises! Try these Signs anyway.

Table 11-4	Ailments		
English	*Sign*	*English*	*Sign*
BREATHING PROBLEM (ASTHMA)		BRUISE	

English	Sign	English	Sign
COUGH		BROKEN BONE	
INFECTION		PAIN/ HURT	
SICK/DISEASE		SORE THROAT	

If you sign **blue** or **purple** and circle the area with your index finger, it means the area is **bruised.**

The Signs in Table 11-5 are the perfect relief. Practice them and you'll feel a whole lot better!

Table 11-5		Remedies	
English	*Sign*	*English*	*Sign*
BEDREST/ REST		CAST	
CRUTCHES		PRESCRIPTION	
WHEELCHAIR			

Cast is signed by making the manual C handshape and placing it on your passive arm in a double sliding motion. If the cast is on a leg, point to the area. If it's a body cast, fingerspell C-A-S-T or else you'll be pointing all day.

You sign **prescription** with the manual letters R-X, and then sign a square with both index fingers starting at the top and meeting at the bottom — it means "slip."

If you're feeling up to it, try the following sentences.

English: She has an infection.
Sign: INFECTION — HAS HER

English: Sit in the wheelchair.
Sign: WHEELCHAIR — SIT

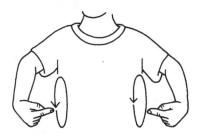 

English: You have a sprain.
Sign: SPRAIN — HAVE YOU

Pointing to Body Parts

If you're using ASL to describe ailments, it helps to be able to do more than point to the part that hurts, although in many cases, that's exactly how you Sign different body parts. Tables 11-6, 11-7, and 11-8 run down the Signs for body parts in three different groups. Most of the Signs in these tables are signed with a double motion; for example, for **ear,** tug twice on your earlobe.

Table 11-6		Parts of Your Head	
English	*Sign*	*English*	*Sign*
EAR		EYE	
HEAD		JAW	
MOUTH		NOSE	
THROAT		TEETH	

Table 11-7	Bendy Places: Joints		
English	*Sign*	*English*	*Sign*
ANKLE		ELBOW	
HIP		KNEE	
KNUCKLE		NECK	
WRIST			

Table 11-8		Larger Body Parts	
English	*Sign*	*English*	*Sign*
ARM		BUTTOCKS	
CHEST		FOOT/FEET	
HAND		LEG	

English	Sign	English	Sign
STOMACH		TORSO/TRUNK	

When you're not feeling that well, these sentences will help you get all the sympathy your hands can hold.

English: My throat is red.
Sign: MY THROAT — RED

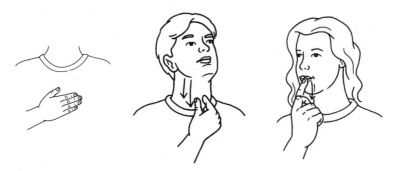

English: My neck is stiff.
Sign: MY NECK — STIFF

You sign stiff by using the same Sign as freeze (see Chapter 6).

English: Can you cough?
Sign: COUGH — CAN YOU Q

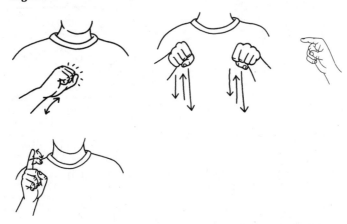

English: Her mouth is bleeding.
Sign: MOUTH BLEEDING — HER

Handling Emergencies

Going to the hospital during an emergency is a scary thing. However, there's nothing scary about these emergency-related Signs (except having to use them). Table 11-9 may be your 9-1-1 when you need to help out in an emergency!

Table 11-9	Emergency Room Talk		
English	*Sign*	*English*	*Sign*
ADMIT/ ENTER		AMBULANCE	
EMERGENCY		HEMORRHAGE/ BLEED	
HOSPITAL		DISCHARGE	

Hemorrhage is the same Sign as **bleed.** To sign bleed, let your dominant hand motion up and down rapidly. The faster you do it, the heavier the bleeding.

Signin' the Sign

Lily and George are going to the hospital; he is ill and needs medical attention. Read on and see how the story unravels:

Lily: You need to get to the hospital.
Sign: HOSPITAL — GO — MUST YOU

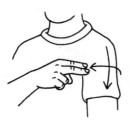 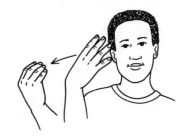

George: I'm dizzy and my stomach hurts.
Sign: DIZZY ME — STOMACH HURTS MINE

 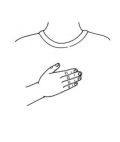

Lily: We'll go to the ER.
Sign: E-R — GO US — WILL

 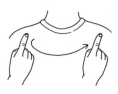 

Fun & Games

This game focuses on Signs that you're likely to need in a medical situation. Fill in the blank with the English word for each medical Sign. The answers are in Appendix A if you need them.

1. Sit down when you're feeling _____.

2. Go to the _____ when you're sick.

3. Gargle when you have a sore _____.

4. Before the nurse _____, make a fist.

5. Don't eat or drink anything the night before _____.

6. When you break your arm, you'll need a _____.

7. A medical _____ needs immediate attention.

8. The doctor's _____ is usually his nurse.

1.
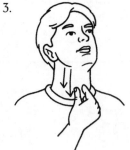

2.

3.

4.

5.

6.

7.

8.

Part IV

Looking into Deaf Life

"You don't have to shout the words out once you know what they are, Derek. This is American Sign Language, not charades."

In this part . . .

*T*his part gives you a glimpse of the Deaf world — their customs, culture, and how they interact, both in our world and their own. The three main topics covered here are the Deaf way of life, Deaf etiquette, and communication devices for the Deaf.

Chapter 12

The Deaf Way

You probably picked up this book because you want to find out how to sign and communicate with Deaf friends, family members, or colleagues. But there's more to the Deaf community than just Sign language. In this chapter, you find out the history of Sign, the challenges that Deaf people have faced both past and present, and what it means to live in two cultures and to speak two languages. This information can help you better understand just what it means to be Deaf, which, in turn, can help you to better communicate with the Deaf people you know.

Many people who can hear typically think Deaf people have a huge void in their lives because they can't hear. Nothing could be further from the truth. Even though Deaf people experience life a bit differently, they have a wonderful quality of life and enjoy the same things that hearing people do.

Digging into Sign's Past

You can find Sign languages in every country throughout the world. Some countries, such as Canada and the United States, have similar Sign languages because their spoken languages are also similar. However, this isn't always the case. American Sign Language (ASL) is unique among the world's Sign languages because it has had many influences and has influenced many Sign languages of the world. This section explains the history of Sign language and the effect that these Sign languages have had on the origins of ASL.

Looking at the origins of Sign language

The roots of Sign language run fairly deep. Although early Greek writings refer to manual communication, no one knows whether those writings refer to just a few gestures or an actual alternative language using Signs. Hippocrates studied deafness, and Socrates believed that it was a natural occurrence for Deaf people to communicate manually.

Juan Pablo Benet (1579–1629) wrote the first book, published in 1620, on how to teach Deaf people. He incorporated gestures, fingerspelling, writing, and speech.

Exploring the two schools of thought on Deaf communication

Throughout history, people have attempted to teach Deaf people language. Many people believed that Deaf people would be enlightened by sound and speech reading. However, others — many of them Deaf — believed that manual communication was a more natural way to express ideas. Two schools of thought evolved regarding the communication methods of Deaf people:

✔ **Oralist method:** This method starts at childhood and relies on residual hearing, speech reading, and speech production in hopes of teaching verbal skills. In many cases, signing is forbidden. This school dates back to Europe. In Edinburgh, Scotland, the Briarwood Academy — perhaps the oldest oral school in Europe — emphasized speech; those who could afford it sent their children to this school. Their method of teaching was unknown because of their policy of secrecy. In America, oralists established themselves in the classroom after the Civil War. With the rebuilding of America, oralists wanted Deaf people to depend on speech rather than Sign language.

Many forms of Sign language, both early and modern, fall under the oralist method school of thought. This approach to Sign language is closely tied to the spoken language of the land. When using the oral method, the signed language adopts the properties of the spoken language. They share a common word order, cultural implications, and idioms. In short, the signed language is a reflection of the spoken language.

Great Britain, Australia, and Russia are some of the countries that use oral methods for communication. Efforts in America have had some success. Alexander Graham Bell was one of the American pioneers. His support of oral methods of teaching gave credibility to oralism. His belief that Deaf children could learn to communicate verbally found a great deal of support from parents who wanted their Deaf children to speak. He was a contributor to schools that were established under this philosophy. A.G. Bell schools are well established in the United States even today.

✔ **Manualism:** Manualism, which emphasizes Sign language over speech, dates back farther than oralism in America. It wasn't until the latter part of the nineteenth century that lip-reading and speech was introduced into the classroom. Instructors of Deaf children believed that education should be done in Sign. Many of these instructors were religious people who believed that Sign language was a gift from God. They believed that the oralists were depriving Deaf children of their natural language.

Examining when and how ASL began

The origin of *American Sign Language* (ASL) has two parts. Many people believe that ASL was strongly influenced by the work of Thomas Hopkins Gallaudet and Laurent Clerc in the early 1800s at the American Asylum in Hartford, Connecticut.

Another influence of ASL's origin goes back long before the arrival of Gallaudet and Clerc. In the seventeenth century, Deaf people were living in the United States. They lived in their own communities on Martha's Vineyard and made their livings as farmers and fishermen. Most of these inhabitants were descendants of people who'd moved to America from England. Three hundred years later, their descendants were still living there and attending the Hartford Asylum under Clerc and Gallaudet. Many believe that the Signs brought to America by these educators and the Signs used by the Vineyard population are largely responsible for today's ASL.

ASL isn't related to English, although it borrows from English — as many spoken languages do. ASL has a word order that's different from English, and it has its own idioms, jokes, and poetry — all unrelated to English. People who support ASL believe that anything can be taught in ASL because it's a language guided by properties.

Sign Language is visually based. An object, such as a person, animal, or thing, needs to be understood by two parties before any information can be signed concerning the subject. Some people believe that this is the natural process for language. Many languages are based on this idea — it's the noun-verb rule. You need to name an object before you can discuss it.

Facing the Challenges of the Deaf Community

Through the years, Deaf people have had to face numerous challenges. In the past, they had little access to education, and almost no opportunity for gainful employment. Although things have improved over time, Deaf people still face challenges. This section discusses challenges past and present and looks at how the Deaf community has made strides to overcome them.

Putting the past behind us

Sign language, like the Deaf people who use it, has had to fight for survival. Around the world, Sign language — as well as those who communicate this way — has been viewed as lesser than that of the hearing world. Many hearing people have dedicated themselves to changing the Deaf and their language.

For centuries, Deaf people had to undergo the treatment of being viewed as incomplete because of their absence of hearing. Some religious groups wanted to *save* Deaf people, while other groups wanted to *teach* them. Because of a lack of speech, Deaf people were viewed as deaf and dumb. This label, which Aristotle invented, has been attached to the Deaf people since ancient Greece.

Deaf people have been associated with being demon-possessed because some of them can't speak. Due to numerous biblical verses labeling them as dumb and mute, the Middle Ages — a dogmatic religious time — wasn't kind to Deaf people. Deaf individuals were hidden by family members, locked in asylums, or forced to try speaking, even though they couldn't hear themselves.

During World War II, Adolf Hitler's henchmen castrated Deaf men after they were locked up in concentration camps as part of various medical experiments.

Contemporary religious leaders have attempted to heal Deaf people of their "sickness" and accused them of lacking faith when miraculous hearing didn't happen.

Some people mock Signing in front of Deaf people or tell them how sorry they are that they can't hear the birds singing or the phone ringing. Others are so rude as to talk about Deaf people right in front of them as though they aren't even there.

Many Deaf people and Deaf advocates have risen to challenge this oppression, and they seem to have been successful because Deaf people are still signing to one another every day.

You've come a long way, baby

Although Deaf people aren't viewed as being possessed by the devil anymore, they still continue to face the challenges presented to them by a hearing world. Deaf people have fought for equal opportunities in education and employment and for cultural recognition, just to name a few. Take a look at how the Deaf community has overcome modern obstacles.

The laws of the land

The Americans with Disabilities Act (ADA) has been a milestone, not only for Deaf people but also for all Americans. Here is some basic information about the ADA. This is not intended to be legal advice but general information. To learn more about the ADA, go on the Internet and search for *Americans with Disabilities*.

Title I: Employment. If 15 employees are deaf or disabled, the workplace must be modified to be accessible. For example, TTYs (see Chapter 14), ramps, and/or railings could be installed.

Title II: Public Services. Programs, activities, and transportation can't discriminate against disabled people. Buses, taxis, and other public means of transportation need to accommodate the disabled population. Programs such as job training, educational classes, and other assistance to gainful employment must also be provided.

Title III: Public Accommodations. All new construction of establishments such as hotels, grocery stores, retail stores, and restaurants are mandated to add physical assistance, such as ramps and railings.

Title IV: Telecommunications. Telecommunication agencies that provide phone services must provide a relay service for TTY users.

Title V: Miscellaneous. Prohibits any threats to disabled people or to persons assisting the disabled.

Getting classified as an "official" language

Although the Deaf population in America has had much progress through laws promoting civil equality and educational advancement of Deaf people, the road to total equality is still a long one. Not all states in America recognize ASL as an actual language.

The dispute over whether ASL is an actual language has been ongoing. Those who think that it should be considered a language often cite the following reasons:

- ✔ It syntactically contains properties like other languages, such as nouns, verbs, and adjectives.
- ✔ It maintains grammar rules that must be followed.

Presently, approximately 20 states support this argument and recognize ASL as a foreign language. In addition, numerous colleges and universities offer credits for ASL as a foreign language.

On the other hand, many people don't buy the argument that ASL is a real language. Their argument goes like this:

- ✔ All countries, including the United States, use their own indigenous sign language. Therefore, if you were from Spain and traveled to Peru, your Spanish Sign Language wouldn't be compatible with Peruvian Sign Language, even though the hearing communities from both countries could speak Spanish and understand each other.

- ✔ At best, some countries, such as the United States, have had a profound impact educationally on other countries. Many foreign Deaf people come to the United States for schooling, and they take home many ASL signs.

Standardizing a Sign language internationally has not happened with any one national Sign language. However, there is a Sign language system called International Sign Language (ISL); it was previously called *Gesturo*. It's used at international Deaf events and conferences. It uses various signs from several national Sign languages and was first used in the 1970s at the World Federation of the Deaf in Finland. To get more information about ISL, contact Gallaudet University.

Living and working as part of the silent minority

In a real sense, Deaf people living in America are a silent minority. The majority is made up of those who can hear. For Deaf people, living in a world where one's language is known by few and understood by even fewer influences how Deaf people view themselves. (To categorize how Deaf people view themselves is too big a label to put on people who are individuals with various educational, economic, social, and deafness levels. Some people are more adaptable than others — in both the hearing and Deaf worlds.)

It also influences their feelings about how to exist as a people. This experience is often compared to living in a foreign country. Think about it: How would you feel if you were living in a foreign land where the language, customs, and culture weren't native to you? You'd probably go through each day with reluctance and uncertainty. You'd want to say what's appropriate, not something that would be viewed as ignorant. You'd feel frustrated when you wanted to state your opinion but couldn't make yourself understood. You'd feel isolated when everyone was laughing at a joke, and you didn't understand the punch line. Deaf people often feel this way when they're surrounded by hearing people.

When speakers of a minority group come together, apart from the majority, they feel a certain sense of freedom to be able to speak — or sign — as fast as they want, and to converse, using idioms in their native language.

The Deaf as an Ethnic Group

Deaf people are an ethnic group. Although they don't share a commonality of skin color, they share a common bond of culture. If culture is defined as a shared knowledge, experience, language, beliefs, and customs, Deaf people are definitely an ethnic group.

This self-awareness of a Deaf ethnic group has only been in existence since the twentieth century. Deaf pride has come from this identification. These people view themselves as whole people, not people with broken ears as the label "hearing impaired" implies. When a person is culturally Deaf, he will identify and sometimes introduce himself as Deaf. To be a member of a Deaf community, the ability to communicate in ASL is a basic requirement.

Understanding Deaf culture

Just like any other culture, the Deaf community has its own customs, beliefs, and arts that are passed down from generation to generation. The culture of the Deaf community isn't arbitrary; it's a system of understandings and behaviors. This cultural group shares the characteristics of other cultural groups:

✔ They share the commonalities of language and the obstacles of daily life.

✔ The Deaf culture is based on a collective mindset, not an individual one. Many Deaf people feel a stronger tie to other Deaf people than to people who can hear.

✔ Deaf people feel a strong bond to one another; they have a strong sense of cooperation.

✔ Deaf people come from all walks of life, from executives to construction workers, and as it is in English, those who are more educated than others are able to communicate more clearly by following the rules of their respective language.

✔ As with all cultures, time modifies and alters some aspects of the culture. This happens because culture is both learned and shared among a given group of people.

Culture teaches members of a community how they, as a people, respond to other ethnic groups and the world around them.

Knowing who falls into the Deaf cultural community

You may be thinking that the question of who fits into the Deaf community is a silly one — Deaf people, obviously! But the Deaf community includes these people, too:

- ✔ Hearing people. Those who can hear play important roles in the community of the Deaf as educators, ASL teachers, and interpreters for the Deaf. Many hearing people are also married to Deaf people or have Deaf children, making them part of the Deaf community.

- ✔ *Children of Deaf Adults* (CODAs). We say "children" because of the acronym, but obviously the term simply means people who have Deaf parents.

Living as bilingual/bicultural people

In order to be successful members of society, Deaf people have to be able to live and communicate in both the Deaf and the hearing worlds. They have to be comfortable with navigating between the two — in other words, they have to be bilingual and bicultural. Proving that Deaf people can live as a bilingual, bicultural people, more Deaf people are attending college, more interpreter training programs are being implemented, and more Deaf people than ever are working in white-collar jobs. Read the following examples to see this dual culture in action.

- ✔ Many Deaf people have felt the burden of not having the spiritual satisfaction that people desire because most churches don't have anyone who knows Sign language to interpret and minister to a Deaf member of the congregation. Today, however, many Deaf people are going into the ministry and leading their own Deaf congregations. Many hearing ministries are also learning ASL.

  The Los Angeles Church of Christ's evangelist, Ron Hammer, learned Sign language from Deaf members of the church. He trained these members in leadership, and the interpreters began an interpreter-training program inside the church. Today, the Deaf membership of that church has increased dramatically to become one of the largest Deaf congregational regions in Los Angeles.

✔ Because Deaf people and hearing people share common interests and topics of conversation, they can use these commonalities to communicate and become closer. When a Deaf person is with his Deaf friends, he may talk about Deaf schools, but he can just as easily converse with a colleague at work about schools in general.

Topics such as the weather, sports, food, and entertainment are all popular (and are all discussed in various chapters of this book) with Deaf people as well as the hearing. Even topics that at first seem unique to the Deaf community are really similar to topics that would be discussed by hearing people. For instance, Deaf people often discuss the nuances of ASL and "play on signs." Hearing people do the same when they play on words, making jokes and puns. Deaf people often converse about schools for the Deaf, discussing which ones they attended and their similar experiences with dorm life and residential supervision. Hearing people also talk about where they went to school, what they majored in, what dorm life was like, and so on.

✔ Politics is a topic of conversation, the same as hearing people. Deaf people are also trying to make sense of political affairs as they, too, have family members who are in the military in these troubled times.

✔ Deaf people also enjoy the company of significant others. Conversations about dates, marriage, disagreements, and making up are topics most people, Deaf or hearing, have in common. Problems and solutions in relationships cross all cultural and linguistic barriers.

Chapter 13

Deaf Etiquette

*J*ust like all other groups of people, the Deaf have reasons for certain norms. Bringing this to life and understanding social norms gives you a better understanding of Deaf etiquette and makes the language of the Deaf people become clear.

Deaf etiquette refers to behaviors that are acceptable norms to the Deaf community. This chapter helps you understand the ways of the Deaf, their nuances, and their customs, as well as the reasons behind them. As you read through this chapter, you find out how to participate in the Deaf world, which allows you to appreciate the complex and silent world that lives around you.

Being Sensitive to Being Deaf

This part of Deaf etiquette is really for the hearing. Deaf people already know what it means to be Deaf, but those who can hear probably never think about the day-to-day struggles that the Deaf have to overcome in this world.

Getting close to a Deaf person requires a little vulnerability on both sides. Many Deaf people are just as insecure about not being understood as you are, but most of them are patient and incredibly skilled at getting their point across to you. Like all people, the Deaf come from all walks of life. Deaf men and women have the same careers that hearing people do — they're doctors, lawyers, teachers, homemakers, construction workers, and so on.

Living together in a hearing world

Here are some tips and hints to keep in mind when interacting with Deaf people:

✔ As your signing progresses, a Deaf person may ask if your parents are Deaf. This is a high compliment about your signing. It doesn't mean that you're fluent in ASL, but it does mean that your signing or facial expressions have characteristics of being influenced by someone who's a native Signer.

✔ When visiting Deaf people, don't assume that you can just walk into the house since they can't hear the doorbell. Deaf people have strobe lights connecting the doorbell to the phone. When either one rings, a light will flash. One light is inside by the door; the other is in a lamp by the phone.

✔ If you're out to a meal with a Deaf person, don't feel obligated to order for them unless you're asked, even if it's just to practice your Sign. Deaf people have been eating in restaurants longer than you've been friends, and they're accustomed to pointing to an item on the menu for the server.

✔ As you learn more Signs, do your best to sign when you're talking with your hearing friends and a Deaf person joins the conversation. It may be hard to sign what you're saying, but you'll be able to do it in time with practice. It'll help the Deaf person feel included if he or she knows what you're saying.

Getting the Deaf perspective

After reading this book, no doubt you see that knowing Sign is just one piece (albeit a large one) of the puzzle to understanding the Deaf community. To really get a grasp on Deaf etiquette and culture, you have to get involved with the Deaf community. One sure way to get involved is to take an introductory Sign Language course from a Deaf instructor. Although you can find some awesome Sign instructors who can hear, a Deaf Sign instructor can teach from the Deaf perspective and may very possibly be a native Signer.

An introductory class gives you exposure to Signs, interaction with others and, hopefully, an opportunity to learn from Deaf guest speakers. You also get an understanding of the many Signing styles that different people possess. An instructor can guide you as to where Deaf activities are taking place, who Deaf community leaders might be, and issues concerning your local community. Consider this class to be a passport to the Deaf community.

Participating in the Deaf Community

We can say a lot about this subject. A good rule to follow is, "When in Rome, do as the Romans do." In other words, when you're with Deaf people, respect their customs; what you don't know, you can figure out by observation and through asking questions. Basically, just watch and learn. Some of the things you may notice include the following:

- ✔ **A sense of unity:** Depending on the size of the Deaf community, Deaf people will congregate at activities such as bowling leagues, Deaf clubs, Deaf plays, and fundraisers. In Los Angeles, California, the Deaf community is very large. Subgroups inside the community consist of Russians, Chinese, Italians, Hispanics, and Jews, not to mention many others. Each of these groups has its own respective traditions, customs, and celebrations. As a whole community, they come together for events such as the Lotus Festival, Deaf West Theater, and Deaf Awareness Month.

- ✔ **ASL pride:** Deaf people speak of ASL quite often in conversations. You may attend plays and parties where ASL is the main topic. The Deaf community is very proud and protective of this language, so it's often a hot topic.

- ✔ **Signing speed:** When you watch Deaf people in conversation and you can't understand anything that is signed, don't lose heart. Novice Signers often don't understand Deaf nuances and abbreviations, and they often have a hard time keeping up. Stay with ASL; before you know it, you'll be signing like a pro.

And, just so you know, few things are more volatile in the Deaf world than a hearing person who, having taken a semester or two of Sign Language classes, proceeds to lecture a Deaf person because he or she doesn't sign the way the Sign Language teacher instructed.

Being aware of Deaf Awareness Month

Deaf Awareness Month, which takes place in September, is nationally recognized and celebrated by the Deaf in their respective communities all across the United States. Each community works closely with the local interpreters to schedule their own events. Some events include picnics, lectures on Deafness, workshops on the Americans with Disabilities Act (where they speak on Deaf rights in the workforce), and the use of interpreters. Fundraisers and raffles are a big hit, too. They help provide resources for scholarships and general assistance to other organizations for the advancement of both Deaf and hearing people alike. If you want to find information regarding Deaf Awareness Month, go to www.rid.org and click on your state's link. Most local chapters publish a monthly calendar.

Corporate organizations, some with a large Deaf staff, also sponsor events. One popular event is Movie Night. Often, a local movie theater will host a recently released movie — with subtitle captioning — at a discounted rate. (Some theaters continue to host special movie nights for the Deaf community throughout the year; check with your local theaters to see if any of them do.)

Another favorite activity during Deaf Awareness Month is the baseball game. For example, the Deaf arrive in droves at the San Diego Padres and L.A. Dodgers games in California. The billboards at the parks even flash a welcome to the Deaf community. Although the games are great, most Deaf people are there to socialize. They do ask who won at the end of the game, though!

The ins and outs of hanging out with Deaf friends

In order to be comfortable in the Deaf community, you should be familiar with some of their customs and nuances. Here are some common customs you may encounter.

Getting someone's attention

You can get a Deaf person's attention in a variety of ways. Each way is used according to the situation. A good general rule is to watch how and when the Deaf people do each one.

- **Flickering the lights:** If you attend a Deaf function and see someone flickering the lights on and off, don't be in a hurry to tell him or her to "knock it off." Flickering the lights gets everyone's attention. This custom is equivalent to yelling for everyone to "listen up." You can also use it to draw attention to yourself when you enter a room in which a Deaf person has his or her back turned toward you.

  It isn't customary to walk up behind a Deaf person and grab, poke, or slap him or her on the back. Doing so isn't necessarily offensive, but that action is used as more of a warning that something is wrong or that there's an emergency.

- **Waving:** Another way to get a Deaf person's attention is to wave your hand in his or her peripheral vision field. Wave casually; a frantic wave may give the impression something is wrong.

- **Tapping:** If you're close enough in distance to the person, a tap on the arm is a sure way to get a response. This is the preferred way to get someone's attention.

- **Pounding and stomping:** Pounding an object, such as a table or counter, and/or stomping on the floor are two more ways that are sometimes used to get attention if someone has his or her back to you. These actions release vibrations that the Deaf person can feel. There's no clear rule to follow as to which method to use, nor do Deaf people show a preference for one over the other. Stomping on the floor is usually done in a one-on-one situation, not in a group setting. You don't need to pound or stomp hard; you just want to get that person's attention, not scare him.

The eyes have it

Deaf people sometimes use their eyes for pointing. This is called *eye-gazing*. Deaf people also stare to refer to someone who isn't present. If you want more info on this topic, flip back to Chapter 3.

Leaving egos at the door

If you're a novice Signer and an invitation is extended to you from a Deaf person, the first rule is: Enjoy yourself! You were invited because that person wants a friendship and/or wants to introduce you to other members of the Deaf community.

Don't make the same mistake that many novice Signers have made: feeling insulted. For people who can hear, having a Deaf person correct your Signing can be frustrating, even insulting. After all, you're trying your best, and although you may not be signing perfectly, you've still received your share of compliments.

They may even see you signing and applaud you with their pinky fingers! In all actuality, they're just having fun with you — not at you. It's their way of giving you encouragement; they're poking fun at you but also sending you a message that your Signing has improved. When they correct your every Sign, they view you as being worthy of the time they spend to do it. When they clap with their pinkies, it means your progress is noticeable, but you're not quite there yet. Any way you look at it, your Deaf friends see something in you that makes them feel good.

Cracking the code

You may also notice Deaf people silently signing together, but when you enter the room, they begin to use their voices. This action is known as *code switching*. The purpose of this is to include you in their conversation, so it's really a compliment.

Facing the door

You may notice that many Deaf people in offices have their desks facing the door, so they can see right away if someone enters the room. If they have computers, their desks may even be a little lower than normal. This is done to enable them to Sign more easily to people on the other side of the desk.

Another problem novice Signers have is trying to keep up with Deaf conversations. The first instinct is to ask the Deaf person to slow down, but that's actually the wrong way to go about it. The Deaf converse at a pace that is normal for Sign. Your eyes need to get used to following the action. If you get lost somewhere in the conversation, that's okay. Don't be embarrassed if someone asks if you understand; repeat what you think you understood. Honesty is honesty in any language.

Patience and practice will be your best friends. You'll get the hang of it soon enough.

Questions you shouldn't ask

Never initiate a conversation about a Deaf person's hearing loss. Questioning someone about this implies that you don't view that person as whole, but broken, incomplete, or inferior. You'll find that the Deaf are comfortable talking about their hearing aids, batteries that need replaced, and ear molds, but it's best if you leave this subject to the individual who has the disability. If you view a Deaf person with equality and respect, the hearing loss won't become a subject of any great importance. Often, as you become better friends, your questions will get answered in a passing conversation.

Just to satisfy your immediate curiosity, most Deaf people do not have a total hearing loss. They usually have what's called *residual hearing,* hearing that remains after deafness occurs, either at birth, after an illness or accident, or because of age. Deaf people have varying degrees of deafness; some are more profoundly deaf than others, so some Deaf people can speak intelligibly while others can't.

In your time with the Deaf, make it a growing experience; you're encountering a people with a rich history, a proud people with a bond of community. You aren't the first person to want to know their language, and you won't be the last.

Someone's in the kitchen with Dinah

At social gatherings in someone's home, it's not uncommon for everyone to gather around the kitchen table. They do this because kitchens typically have good lighting, allowing everyone to see the Signs clearly.

Chapter 14

Talking on the Phone

• •

In This Chapter

▶ Conversing on the phone

▶ Relaying through the operator

▶ Paging the deaf

▶ Using a sign language interpreter

• •

*F*or most of us, making a phone call is as easy as picking up the phone and dialing. This hasn't always been the case for members of the Deaf community, though. Deaf people didn't get to share in the success of the invention of the telephone until much later.

In this chapter, we look at different communication devices and services that have been invented to be user-friendly for the Deaf consumer. We also explain some devices that are currently used by both Deaf and hearing people. These machines are used to communicate with people next door, across town, or across the country. In both the Deaf and hearing worlds, technology is constantly changing. What we use today for communication may be obsolete tomorrow. Today, videophones and video relay services, tomorrow, who knows? We also clue you in as to how to use them, so that you can be sure to stay in touch with Deaf friends and family no matter where you are.

Teletypes (TTYs) for the Deaf

Although Alexander Graham Bell and his associates ushered the telephone into existence in 1875, the first teletype machine wasn't invented until 1964 — nearly 100 years later. It was invented by a deaf physicist named Robert Weitbrecht. With this invention, Weitbrecht opened up the world of tele-conversation to the Deaf.

CULTURAL WISDOM

When people refer to teletype machines, they may refer to them as TTYs (TeleTYpe) or as TDDs (Telecommunications Device for the Deaf). The term TDD came after TTY. Both terms are acceptable, but Deaf people themselves are more apt to use TTY over TDD; they view TDD as a term created by hearing people.

The TTY is a combination of a teletype machine and a telephone. The keyboard of the TTY sends a series of beeps with each letter. These letters are printed across a screen above the keyboard. Some TTYs, but not all, come equipped with text paper that automatically records your conversation. TTYs can be purchased through phone companies or through businesses that specialize in telecommunications. Many Deaf people receive TTYs from the Department of Vocational Rehabilitation. This agency will purchase TTYs for the deaf consumer to do "whatever services are necessary and appropriate to succeed in employment." Deaf people are provided TTYs at no cost by some states.

To use the TTY, you place the handle of the phone on the "cups" of the TTY — the earpiece of the receiver always goes on the cup to the right. Dial the phone number of your intended party and wait for it to ring. The light on the TTY machine will flash as the phone is ringing. The party at the other end will start typing as soon as they put their receiver on their TTY cups.

If someone gives you a business card that has "V/TTY" or "V/TDD" next to a phone number, this means that the phone number has both voice and teletype capabilities.

Certain abbreviations are used when conversing on the TTY. Table 14-1 lists some standard TTY terms.

Table 14-1	Common Terms		
Abbreviation	*Meaning*	*Abbreviation*	*Meaning*
ok	okay	crs	(any state) relay service
msg/e	message	asst.	assist
ur	your	thx	thanks
shd	should	ltrs	letters
biz	business	btw	by the way
oic	oh, I see	pls	please
u	you	r	are
nbr	number	misc	miscellaneous
tmw	tomorrow	cn	can
cul	see you later	sk sk	hanging up
ga	go ahead (signals it's the other person's turn to talk)		

TTYs go public

Thanks to the *Americans with Disabilities Act* (ADA), TTYs and other devices for the disabled can now be found in hospitals, police stations, airports, and the like. On July 26, 1990, legislation was passed stating that telecommunications companies that provide phone services to the general public must also provide a relay service for people who use TTYs. So, deaf people can have TTYs accessible to them when the need arises. If any agency or organization violates the law, the federal government can impose a fine.

A TTY Conversation

Mike and Mark are chatting on the TTY (phone) about a car show. Notice how they converse using TTY etiquette.

Mike: Q hey enjoy the cr show ga
English: Hey, did you enjoy the car show?

Mark: Yes, Q want to go tmw ga
English: Yes. Do you want to go tomorrow?

Mike: No I hv an appt ga
English: No, I have an appointment.

Mark: oic, ok, I'll call u ltr ga
English: Oh, I see. Okay, I'll call you later.

Mike: Great take care ga sk sk
English: Great. Take care.

Mark: sk sk

Here are a few tips on TTY usage:

- ✔ **Don't interrupt a person while he's typing; allow him to give you a "go ahead" (GA).** Interrupting someone during a typical phone conversation may be rude, but doing so doesn't cause the phone to malfunction. On the TTY, though, taking turns is necessary because the TTY has sound activation tones (beeps) that are converted to letters that are punched from the keyboard. If two people try talking at the same time, the sentences won't appear coherently.

- ✔ **If you make an error, just type "XXX" next to the sentence that you want to erase.** If you make a small typo of just a letter or word, though, use the delete or backspace key like usual.

> ✔ **Don't be shy about expressing your emotions.** Words such as smile, grin, ha-ha, and others can be added to the end of your sentence for emphasis.

Relying on Relay Services

Relay service is just that — a telephone service that relays information to a caller who doesn't have or isn't using a TTY. A toll-free number connects you to a TTY operator. You can find this number in the front section of any phone book under Directory Services or from any agency that provides services for the Deaf or hard-of-hearing. The relay service is also extended to the speech-disabled.

You can choose one of many numbers when using the relay service. Just pick the one that will best suit your needs:

> ✔ One number is a voice number that a hearing person uses to call another TTY user or a TTY number that a Deaf caller can dial to contact a relay operator to call someone who doesn't have a TTY. Each state has a different number.

> ✔ Another one is a three digit number, 711, that will connect a non-TTY caller to any state's relay service.

> ✔ TTY users can call the *Operator Services for the Deaf* (OSD) for directory assistance at 800-885-4000. All states have their own relay service.

> ✔ To call the relay internationally, dial 605-224-1837.

Relay service operators are usually very skilled typists, although we've experienced a couple of them who were slower than snails with sprained ankles! Don't be intimidated by the relay service. Actually, after you've used the relay service a few times and experienced how time-consuming a three-way conversation can be, you'll want to get your own TTY.

Using a relay service

When you call the voice operator, the first thing the operator will say is, "This is operator _____." You'll then hear the question, "ID number — may I have the number you're calling?" After you give him or her the number, you'll be asked if you've ever used the relay service. If you haven't, a short explanation is given as to what you can expect during the duration of the call. You'll also be told that he or she won't be able to hear you until the person on the other end comes on the line. You can hear the phone ring until it's picked up, but you won't hear the operator identify the relay service and your name to the person you're calling. The operator usually lets the phone ring ten times before coming back on the line to let you know if there was no answer. If you're calling a physically disabled or an elderly Deaf person, however, you may want to ask the operator to let the phone ring longer.

When you do connect with someone on the other end, be sensitive regarding the operator. Most of them are skilled typists, but you may have a tendency to speak faster than the operator can type. Try speaking in segments, listening to the operator's keys. When you hear the typing stop, you know that you can continue speaking.

Speaking privately through a third party

The operators who work for relay services agree to keep the conversations that they hear confidential. We have heard rumors of operators sharing portions of conversations with third parties, but as far as we know, we've never had that experience.

If you have to discuss issues that you feel uncomfortable talking about with an operator who's of the opposite sex, you can request to have an operator of your same sex relay the call — as long as one is available.

Understanding conversations with relay service

The last thing that you need to remember when talking through the relay is that some Deaf people write like they sign. As discussed in previous chapters, English and Sign often don't share the same grammatical rules. The typist will repeat everything verbatim, regardless of who's doing the typing. The typist will repeat exactly what the Deaf person types and then the operator will type exactly what the hearing person says. If you're talking to a Deaf person on the phone, it may be to your advantage to first read through this book to understand the ways of Sign.

Packing Pagers

Another means of communication that has become popular among the Deaf community is the use of pagers. Unlike the hearing, who typically use pagers as a means of obtaining phone numbers with which to call people back, the Deaf community uses pagers to actually communicate back and forth. (This type of communication is similar to the text-messaging that's available on modern cell phones.)

These special pagers, called *two-way pagers,* are a compact version of a regular pager and TTY. They come complete with keyboards, phone directories, e-mail, and scrolling features. You can send a message and get a reply as quickly as it takes someone to type and send it. These pagers can be purchased at most telecommunication organizations, and you can also find them on the Web. They are a bit on the expensive side — often a few hundred dollars — but activation is included in the price. You can also find rebuilt models, which are a little cheaper, but your best bet is to wait for a sale on new models. You might want to look for a good deal on the Internet. Just go to your favorite search engine and type in "Deaf Pagers"; you'll find plenty of information.

Two-way pagers work in regional areas but not necessarily throughout the country.

Another type of pager allows the Deaf person to type a text message into his pager. A relay center from the pager provider will receive the text. They will then call the number per the Deaf person's request and repeat verbatim what the Deaf person wishes to relay. Unfortunately, cell phones don't work with these pager systems.

Using a Tele-Interpreter

Tele-interpreting isn't as common as it used to be. However, not all Deaf people have immediate access to communication devices, and machines tend to break down every now and then. Tele-interpreting, which utilizes the help of Sign Language interpreters, will always be a backup alternative.

Understanding the role of sign language interpreters

A Sign Language interpreter is a person who conveys information from spoken English into *American Sign Language* (ASL) and vice versa.

Many interpreters test for competency certification. Part of the test is understanding and following the code of ethics of sign language interpreters. Confidentiality is the most important part of this code; if an interpreter reveals information that she's learned while interpreting, a formal complaint can be filed with the organization that issues the certification, and that complaint will be investigated.

Most interpreters who are nationally certified have been issued certification from the *Registry of Interpreters for the Deaf* (RID). A certification of competency means that you have satisfied the minimum requirements that have been established. To contact RID, go to www.rid.org, to contact NAD, go to www.nad.org. Certified interpreters from both organizations carry wallet-sized cards of verification. Noncertified interpreters are usually working toward being certified.

Using an interpreter for telephone conversations

Interpreting a phone conversation for a Deaf person is usually done when a Deaf person needs to give or receive information. When the phone is dialed and someone responds, the interpreter signs to the Deaf person that someone has answered. The Deaf person says who he is and that he's speaking through an interpreter. A delay always occurs while the Deaf person is signing and the interpreter is visually reading the signed information. This silence may seem a little awkward, but it's necessary. When the Deaf person is finished, he indicates that the conversation has ended by saying good-bye to the other party.

Another way to tele-interpret is to use an earpiece that's connected to the phone. These are used by Deaf people who have speech capabilities but need an interpreter to receive information. This process is usually done with a Deaf person and a hearing person. The interpreter listens to the conversation through the earpiece and then signs to the Deaf person what the other party is saying. Again, the Deaf person terminates the conversation when he's ready. At no point is the interpreter to intervene with any opinion or advice. The conversation should take place without the interpreter being an active participant in the actual conversation.

Telephone interpreting can become a complicated process if the interpreter begins the process without any foreknowledge of what the Deaf person is trying to accomplish. Most Deaf people let the interpreter know the reason for the call. The Deaf person then dials the number, and the interpreter begins the process.

Fun & Games

Match these abbreviations to their words. Then see if you can decode the TTY sentence into English. You can find the answers in Appendix A.

1. impt		a. Tomorrow
2. sk sk		b. You
3. pls		c. Stop keying
4. tmw		d. Please
5. ga		e. Message
6. msg		f. Important
7. u		g. Go ahead
8. asap		h. As soon as possible

TTY message: Tmw I will have impt msg for U pls respond ASAP GA sk

Part V
The Part of Tens

The 5th Wave   By Rich Tennant

In this part . . .

The three chapters in this part give you helpful and fun ideas to aid you in your quest for using Sign to communicate. Try all the ideas; explore places that you've never been or even knew existed, such as Deaf camps and clubs. Have confidence; ask a lot of questions. You can even have a little fun practicing some of the more popular Deaf idioms on your friends.

Chapter 15

Ten Tips to Help You Sign like a Pro

his chapter is all about providing you with ideas to practice and polish your signing skills. So if you're reading this, you're on the right track.

Watch Yourself and Others Sign

Watching yourself sign while standing in front of a mirror helps you to see what others see when you sign. Watching interpreters lets you see how they make facial expressions and how they use Signs in context. Watching others sign also gives you the opportunity to *read* how they sign. Try videotaping yourself signing and then play it back. You can be your own best critic.

Discover Multiple Signs for Communicating One Thing

One thing can be signed in many different ways. The more ways you know, the more versatile you'll be. Practice signing the variety of ways to mean something. Even if the Sign doesn't suit you, you just may see it again. For example, there are a variety of ways to sign **do.** Ask a person who's been signing for a few years to show them to you.

Practice Your Signing

Practicing is the only way to get comfortable with signing. Practice whenever you're walking, lying in bed, or on your coffee break. Everyone may think that you're a lunatic, but we know the truth! The bottom line: To be a really good signer, signing has to become second nature.

Always Fingerspell a Name First

The Deaf community gives name Signs to people. These name Signs serve as identification. However, a person's name must be established before you can use his or her name Sign or talk about that person. If you don't fingerspell a person's name first, you'll only cause confusion as to whom you mean.

Adjust Your Eyes; Everyone's Signing Is Different

Personalities tend to come out in Sign, just as they do in English. Some people talk fast and sign fast while others want to give you all the details. Just as no two people talk alike, no two Signers sign alike. By being open to the ways that different people sign, you can grow to understand the variety of Signing styles as easily as you can understand most English speakers in the United States.

Facial Expressions Are Like Vocal Inflections

Imagine talking without any high or low pitches — speaking only in a monotone — with few clues to emphasize your point. Your conversation would be boring and hard to understand. The same holds true when you're signing. If you sign about someone being angry, look angry! If you want to convey your joy, you need to show that joy, and if something scary happened to you, look scared! As a general rule, the most clear facial expression is an authentic one. You'll achieve this by practicing actual expressions: Put on a big smile for joy, frown when you want to show sadness or unhappiness, or frown and scrunch your eyebrows together to convey a feeling of anger.

Keep a Journal of Your Great Experiences

Keeping a journal of your adventures in Sign is a great tool. Writing down the signs and styles you've encountered, the time you understood without asking for a repeat, and the first time you could tell someone what others were signing are all noteworthy events. Jotting these things down gives you the perfect way to see your own progress — it should be a great encouragement to you!

Get Some Signing Space

Signing and talking affect where you sit or stand. Because signing is manual, give Signers a little room to converse. If you need privacy, go somewhere private to have your conversation. Make sure that you stand where bright light or the sun isn't directly behind you because whoever is watching you sign will only see your silhouette — a big giveaway that you're just a beginner.

Don't Jump the Gun

Sometimes, when you're watching someone sign, you may lose that person and not understand what is meant. Don't lose heart. Let that person finish the thought; you may put it all together at the very end after all the information has been signed. Then, if you still don't understand, just explain that you didn't catch everything and let that person know what you did catch.

Watch the Face, Not the Hands

You can find most of what you need to know on a Signer's face. A person's face conveys the mood, pauses, any information that can be demonstrated through mouth shapes, and how the action is done (slowly, quickly, sloppily). If you focus on a Signer's hands, you miss a lot of crucial information; instead, focus on the Signer's face and shoulders. Use your peripheral vision to watch the hands. By doing this, you see the whole Signer, and you're apt to better understand the conversation.

Chapter 16

Ten Ways to Pick Up Sign Quickly

Signing with your friends has never been so easy. You have natural Signs and gestures to make your point. You also have this book to add to what you already know. This chapter is short, but it gives you great ideas for some of the things you can do if you want to pick up ASL a little more quickly.

Volunteer at a Residential School for the Deaf

One way to immerse yourself into the Deaf world is to work at a residential school for the Deaf. Deaf culture is the way of life at these schools, and by being exposed to the culture, you become intimately familiar with Sign. You can volunteer in their after-school recreation programs or special-event preparations. Schools can never have too many volunteers to act as score-keepers, coaches, assistants, ticket sellers, or in any other capacity that makes a program a success. By interacting with Deaf students, teachers, and parents, you'll measurably improve both your expressive (signing to others) and receptive (reading others' Signs) signing.

Volunteer at Local Deaf Clubs

Many Deaf people tend to congregate at their own clubs for a variety of reasons. They socialize, play pool, and watch TV, just to name a few activities. Many Deaf people bring their hearing children to these clubs, so that they can practice their signing and learn the ways of the Deaf culture. Some clubs even have photo albums of past members and guests. Deaf clubs also have fundraising events fairly often. Helping at one of these fundraisers is a great opportunity to practice signing while helping others at the same time. Volunteers are always needed to sell raffle tickets, take tickets during an event, keep score at games, or simply serve refreshments.

Attend Deaf Social Functions

Social functions are becoming more common since more Deaf people have started specialized organizations. These events can vary from sports activities to Deaf camp-outs to raffles. People interested in helping with flyers and tickets are always welcome. You can find out about functions in your community by checking the community pages in the phone book, looking on the Internet, or calling the local residential school for the Deaf if your community has one.

Make Deaf Friends

Having Deaf friends is really no different than having hearing friends. Many Deaf people enjoy sports, going shopping, and surfing the Internet. A Deaf friend can help you a lot with ASL. Just think carefully about your friendship, though. Deaf people are sharing a language and culture with you that they hold in high regard — please try to do the same.

Assist Deaf Ministries

Attending Deaf churches and ministries is a sure way to meet Deaf people. Watching religious interpreters in these settings keeps you on the cutting edge of Sign vocabulary. Some churches that have large Deaf ministries have programs set up for members of their congregation who wish to interpret for the Deaf. Church activities, such as picnics and Deaf Bible study groups, are enjoyable areas in which you could offer your assistance.

Attend Deaf Movies and Plays

Many local theaters have weekly plays, which include one night of an interpreted performance. In metropolitan areas, Deaf theaters have plays with all Deaf actors. Some larger cities also have movie nights featuring captioned subtitles. Many Deaf people attend these functions, so they're great avenues for meeting different people and learning about Deaf culture.

Work at Camps for the Deaf

Working at a Deaf camp gives the novice Signer a relaxed atmosphere in which to work with Deaf children. Deaf camps are filled with games, hiking, and other good times. The new Signer has ample opportunity to interact with Deaf people from different areas and to encounter a variety of signing jargon and styles. You may even get the opportunity to see both adults and children perform stories in Sign. Who knows, during a week of camp you may even form new friendships that last long after camp has ended.

Attend Silent Weekends

Silent weekends aren't as lengthy as Deaf camps. Beginning Signers who can't miss time from work may find these weekends a perfect opportunity to mix with the Deaf community. These weekends vary as to how they're run. Some furnish cabins that allow people to talk in the evenings, usually after 4 or 6 p.m., while others allow no talking at all. In fact, you may even be fined — 10 or 25 cents per infraction — if you're caught talking at all. Entertainment is on hand, and an array of ASL teachers and interpreters are there to ensure that the weekend is filled with accurate Signing. You can obtain information about these silent weekends by going to www.rid.org. Each state has a chapter of the *Registry of Interpreters for the Deaf (RID)*. Click on your state's link for information.

Go to Deaf Workshops and Conferences

Many Deaf organizations exist, and one in particular is the *National Association of the Deaf* (NAD). Workshops and conferences take place through these organizations and offer a myriad of subjects — something to interest everyone. One popular subject is Sign itself. Many educators and veteran interpreters regularly present poetry in Sign or give in-depth analyses of particular properties of Sign. Attending one of these workshops may give a beginning Signer a new insight on Deaf aspects.

Watch Sign Language Videos

Videos are a sure way to get your Signing where you want to take it. Many companies specialize in Sign Language materials and will be happy to send you their catalogs. Get together with a Deaf friend, grab a catalog, and let your friend help you decide which videos would be good to learn from based on your particular level of ability. The best way to find sources of these types of videos is to surf the Net. Just enter the words "sign language" into your search engine and watch how many sites come up. Your local library is also a good source for videos — you can often borrow them free of charge. Although books are a big help, videos not only demonstrate three-dimensional Signing but also can be rewound and viewed at a slower-than-normal speed. Besides, viewing one of these videos with a friend can be a lot of fun.

Chapter 17

Ten Popular Deaf Expressions

In This Chapter

▶ Expressing ASL expressions

▶ Understanding when to use them

ASL uses expressions in much the same way that English does. This chapter describes some that are commonly used in Sign. As a helpful hint, practice these expressions with people who've been signing for a while. This can be a shortcut to your success.

Some of the following Signs have an exact English equivalent, and some don't. The ones that don't, however, are quite similar to an English expression.

Swallowed the fish

The idea behind this idiom is right up there with the word **gullible.** You can sign it about yourself or another person. You use it in good humor after someone has mistakenly placed his trust in someone he shouldn't have.

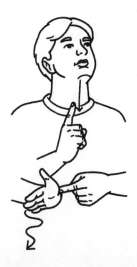

Train gone

You don't normally direct this light-hearted idiom toward yourself, but rather toward someone else. This Sign, which can be compared to the English idiom "missed the boat" is often used when someone tells a joke and everyone is laughing but one person, or when one person wants something repeated that everyone else managed to understand the first time. At these times, someone will look at that person, smile, and sign TRAIN GONE. The facial expression for this Sign may be puffed cheeks (imitating a smokestack) or just a blank stare, whichever you prefer. Either way, everyone will know that someone didn't catch the information.

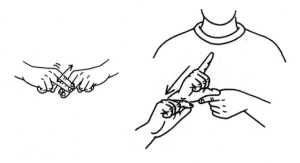

Pea brain

Hearing people use this idiom as well, but just as with English, this is one idiom that you shouldn't use very often because it's not polite. In fact, it's somewhat offensive, although perhaps in a group of good friends you can get away with it if you mean it in good fun. The facial expression that accompanies this Sign determines the degree of meaning or, in this case, maybe the size of one's brain! Sticking your flattened tongue out while signing PEA BRAIN makes it pretty clear as to what you mean. What's even meaner is crossing your eyes while you're doing it. So as a general rule, save it for people you know really well.

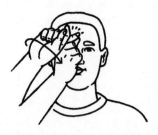

Shucks/Darn!

Make this expression when something didn't go as expected. If you've ever experienced this situation, you'll probably already know how it's used. Like the illustration indicates, you open your passive hand facing up and, using your dominant hand, start with the manual number 5 and with the manual letter S act like you're catching a fly in the palm of your hand.

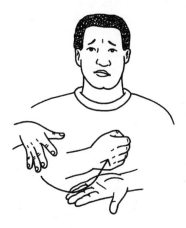

Cross fingers on both hands

Crossing your fingers on both hands is an expression that means **I hope;** it's pretty simplistic and is generally understood in both the hearing and Deaf worlds alike.

Your guess is as good as mine

Again, this Sign is used in English, too. And, as in English, it's only used after someone asks a question. However, in Sign, you can ask a question and use this expression at the same time. A good facial expression to go with it is to smirk (smiling with just the corner of your mouth) and raise your eyebrows. Another way to emphasize this expression is to make the size of the Sign bigger. Doing so tells whomever you're signing to that you really don't have any idea whatsoever.

Cool!

You can sign this expression in one of two ways; both have the same meaning but in different degrees. You use it in response to something communicated to you by another person. Be sure to make the Sign on your chest, leaving your facial expression fully visible — that's where the difference is. Forming an "ooh" shape with your mouth means **really cool.** Opening your mouth wide can mean **a surprised cool.**

5 to manual S under chin

Make this Sign when you witness or express an embarrassing action. Open your eyes wide; you can even put on a nervous smile as you express it. This Sign is done with the manual 5 palm facing the Signer and is closed to make the manual S — it signifies a lump in your throat.

Bent ring finger

By making this Sign, you're saying that someone is ultra-conservative, close-minded, or just an old-fashioned square. Your facial expression is lips pressed tightly together, perhaps paired with a snobbish-type expression.

Crossed index fingers in "X" handshape

This expression is also commonly used in both hearing and Deaf worlds. It's sometimes used when someone sneezes and you want to let that person know that you don't want to catch his or her cold. It can also mean **stay back** or **don't come any closer.**

Part VI
Appendixes

The 5th Wave   By Rich Tennant

SIGNING THE WORD "BABY"

ITALICIZING THE WORD "BABY"

In this part . . .

Appendix A contains all the answers to those tricky Fun & Games questions and puzzles. Appendix B provides detailed instructions for playing and using the CD.

Appendix A

Answer Key to Fun & Games

• •

Chapter 1

Refer to Chapter 1 or the Cheat Sheet for the manual alphabet.

Chapter 2

Answers: 1-g (first); 2-h (Wow); 3-e (six); 4-f (eat); 5-b (big); 6-c (chair, sit); 7-d (fly, planes); 8-a (What — the sign W-T)

Chapter 3

Answers: 1. France 2. angry 3. name 4. hello 5. U.S. 6. Mexico 7. bye

Chapter 4

Answers: 1-d; 2-i; 3-e; 4-h; 5-a; 6-j; 7-c; 8-g; 9-k; 10-b; 11-f; 12-l

Chapter 5

Answers given in chapter.

Chapter 6

Answers: 1-f; 2-h; 3-g; 4-e; 5-b; 6-a; 7-d; 8-c.

Chapter 7

Answers: 1-c; 2-d; 3-g; 4-a; 5-f; 6-b; 7-e

Chapter 8

Answers: 1-a (picnic); 2-e (dark); 3-g (relax); 4-f (gambling); 5-c (baseball); 6-d (game); 7-b (thunder); 8-h (wrestling)

Chapter 9

Answers: a-2 (copy machine); b-1 (computer); c-5 (employees); d-8 (terminated); e-3 (laptop); f-7 (promotions); g-4 (office); h-6 (hire)

Chapter 10

Answers: 1. The bus is late. 2. Where is your car? 3. The train goes north. 4. I ride the subway. 5. Is that your motorcycle? 6. Drive two miles. 7. The tree is near the lake. 8. Turn left at the gas station. 9. Cross the bridge. 10. He lives in the mountains.

Chapter 11

Answers: 1. dizzy; 2. doctor; 3. throat; 4. draws blood; 5. surgery; 6. cast; 7. emergency; 8. assistant

Chapter 14

Answers: 1-f; 2-c; 3-d; 4-a; 5-g; 6-e; 7-b; 8-h

English: Tomorrow I will have an important message for you. Please respond as soon as possible. Go ahead. Stop keying.

Appendix B

About the CD

System Requirements

Make sure that your computer meets the minimum system requirements shown in the following list. If your computer doesn't match up to most of these requirements, you may have problems using the software and files on the CD. For the latest and greatest information, please refer to the ReadMe file located at the root of the CD-ROM.

- A PC with a Pentium or faster processor; or a Mac OS computer with a 68040 or faster processor
- Microsoft Windows 95 or later; or Mac OS system software 7.6.1 or later
- At least 32MB of total RAM installed on your computer; for best performance, we recommend at least 64MB
- A CD-ROM drive
- A monitor capable of displaying at least 256 colors or grayscale
- A modem with a speed of at least 14,400 bps

If you need more information on the basics, check out these books published by Wiley Publishing, Inc.: *PCs For Dummies,* by Dan Gookin; *Macs For Dummies,* by David Pogue; *iMacs For Dummies,* by David Pogue; *Windows 95*

For Dummies, Windows 98 For Dummies, Windows 2000 Professional For Dummies, Microsoft Windows Me Millennium Edition For Dummies, all by Andy Rathbone.

Using the CD with Microsoft Windows

To install from the CD to your hard drive, follow these steps:

1. **Insert the CD into your computer's CD-ROM drive.**

2. **Click the Start button and choose Run from the menu.**

3. **In the dialog box that appears, type** d:\Start.htm.

   Replace *d* with the proper drive letter for your CD-ROM if it uses a different letter. (If you don't know the letter, double-click My Computer on your desktop and see what letter is listed for your CD-ROM drive.)

   Your browser opens, and the license agreement is displayed.

4. **Read through the license agreement, nod your head, and click the Agree button if you want to use the CD.**

   After you click Agree, you're taken to the Main menu, where you can browse through the contents of the CD.

5. **To navigate within the interface, click a topic of interest to take you to an explanation of the files on the CD and how to use or install them.**

6. **To install software from the CD, simply click the software name.**

   You'll see two options: to run or open the file from the current location or to save the file to your hard drive. Choose to run or open the file from its current location, and the installation procedure continues. When you finish using the interface, close your browser as usual.

Note: We have included an "easy install" in these HTML pages. If your browser supports installations from within it, go ahead and click the links of the program names you see. You'll see two options: Run the File from the Current Location and Save the File to Your Hard Drive. Choose to Run the File from the Current Location and the installation procedure will continue. A Security Warning dialog box appears. Click Yes to continue the installation.

To run some of the programs on the CD, you may need to keep the disc inside your CD-ROM drive. This is a good thing. Otherwise, a very large chunk of the program would be installed to your hard drive, consuming valuable hard drive space and possibly keeping you from installing other software.

Using the CD with Mac OS

To install items from the CD to your hard drive, follow these steps:

1. **Insert the CD into your computer's CD-ROM drive.**

   In a moment, an icon representing the CD you just inserted appears on your Mac desktop. Chances are, the icon looks like a CD.

2. **Double-click the CD icon to show the CD's contents.**

3. **Double-click** `start.htm` **to open your browser and display the license agreement.**

   If your browser doesn't open automatically, open it as you normally would by choosing File⇨Open File (in Internet Explorer) or File⇨Open⇨Location in Netscape (in Netscape Navigator) and select *Signing FD*. The license agreement appears.

4. **Read through the license agreement, nod your head, and click the Accept button if you want to use the CD.**

   After you click Accept, you're taken to the Main menu. This is where you can browse through the contents of the CD.

5. **To navigate within the interface, click any topic of interest and you're taken you to an explanation of the files on the CD and how to use or install them.**

6. **To install software from the CD, simply click the software name.**

What You'll Find on the CD

The following sections are arranged by category and provide a summary of the software and other goodies you'll find on the CD. If you need help with installing the items provided on the CD, refer back to the installation instructions in the preceding section.

Shareware programs are fully functional, free, trial versions of copyrighted programs. If you like particular programs, register with their authors for a nominal fee and receive licenses, enhanced versions, and technical support. *Freeware programs* are free, copyrighted games, applications, and utilities. You can copy them to as many PCs as you like — for free — but they offer no technical support. *GNU software* is governed by its own license, which is included inside the folder of the GNU software. There are no restrictions on distribution of GNU software. See the GNU license at the root of the CD for more details. *Trial, demo,* or *evaluation* versions of software are usually limited either by time or functionality (such as not letting you save a project after you create it).

Dialogues

For Windows and Mac.

All the examples provided in this book are located in the dialogues directory on the CD and work with Macintosh and Windows 95/98/NT and later computers. These files contain much of the sample code from the book. The structure of the examples directory is

STS/CDIntro.swf

STS/Chapter1/Alphabet.swf

STS/Chapter2/Numbers.swf

STS/Chapter2/Restaurant.swf

STS/Chapter2/Anniversary.swf

STS/Chapter2/Housevisit.swf

STS/Chapter3/Park.swf

STS/Chapter3/Store.swf

STS/Chapter3/RoadTrip.swf

STS/Chapter4/Roommates.swf

STS/Chapter4/Chicago.swf

STS/Chapter4/Dinnerparty.swf

STS/Chapter6/Shopping.swf

STS/Chapter7/Movies.swf

STS/Chapter8/Weather.swf

STS/Chapter9/House.swf

STS/Chapter10/Directions.swf

STS/Chapter11/Hospital.swf

Shockwave and Flash Player

For Mac and Windows. Commercial version. Enables you to view Macromedia
Flash content. For more information, check out www.macromedia.com.

Troubleshooting

I tried my best to compile programs that work on most computers with the
minimum system requirements. Alas, your computer may differ, and some
programs may not work properly for some reason.

The two likeliest problems are that you don't have enough memory (RAM)
for the programs you want to use, or you have other programs running that
are affecting installation or running of a program. If you get an error message
such as Not enough memory or Setup cannot continue, try one or more
of the following suggestions and then try using the software again:

- **Turn off any antivirus software running on your computer.** Installation
  programs sometimes mimic virus activity and may make your computer
  incorrectly believe that it's being infected by a virus.

- **Close all running programs.** The more programs you have running, the
  less memory is available to other programs. Installation programs typically update files and programs; so if you keep other programs running,
  installation may not work properly.

- **Have your local computer store add more RAM to your computer.** This
  is, admittedly, a drastic and somewhat expensive step. However, if you
  have a Windows 95 PC or a Mac OS computer with a PowerPC chip,
  adding more memory can really help the speed of your computer and
  allow more programs to run at the same time. This may include closing
  the CD interface and running a product's installation program from
  Windows Explorer.

If you still have trouble installing the items from the CD, please call the
Customer Service phone number at 800-762-2974 (outside the U.S.:
317-572-3994) or send e-mail to techsupdum@wiley.com. Wiley Publishing
Inc. will provide technical support only for installation and other general
quality control items; for technical support on the applications themselves,
consult the program's vendor or author.

Vocabulary and General Index

• *D* •

• Q •

• R •

• S •

● *T* ●

Notes

Notes

Wiley Publishing, Inc.
End-User License Agreement

READ THIS. You should carefully read these terms and conditions before opening the software packet(s) included with this book "Book". This is a license agreement "Agreement" between you and Wiley Publishing, Inc. "WPI". By opening the accompanying software packet(s), you acknowledge that you have read and accept the following terms and conditions. If you do not agree and do not want to be bound by such terms and conditions, promptly return the Book and the unopened software packet(s) to the place you obtained them for a full refund.

1. **License Grant.** WPI grants to you (either an individual or entity) a nonexclusive license to use one copy of the enclosed software program(s) (collectively, the "Software," solely for your own personal or business purposes on a single computer (whether a standard computer or a workstation component of a multi-user network). The Software is in use on a computer when it is loaded into temporary memory (RAM) or installed into permanent memory (hard disk, CD-ROM, or other storage device). WPI reserves all rights not expressly granted herein.

2. **Ownership.** WPI is the owner of all right, title, and interest, including copyright, in and to the compilation of the Software recorded on the disk(s) or CD-ROM "Software Media". Copyright to the individual programs recorded on the Software Media is owned by the author or other authorized copyright owner of each program. Ownership of the Software and all proprietary rights relating thereto remain with WPI and its licensers.

3. **Restrictions on Use and Transfer.**

    (a) You may only (i) make one copy of the Software for backup or archival purposes, or (ii) transfer the Software to a single hard disk, provided that you keep the original for backup or archival purposes. You may not (i) rent or lease the Software, (ii) copy or reproduce the Software through a LAN or other network system or through any computer subscriber system or bulletin-board system, or (iii) modify, adapt, or create derivative works based on the Software.

    (b) You may not reverse engineer, decompile, or disassemble the Software. You may transfer the Software and user documentation on a permanent basis, provided that the transferee agrees to accept the terms and conditions of this Agreement and you retain no copies. If the Software is an update or has been updated, any transfer must include the most recent update and all prior versions.

4. **Restrictions on Use of Individual Programs.** You must follow the individual requirements and restrictions detailed for each individual program in the About the CD-ROM appendix of this Book. These limitations are also contained in the individual license agreements recorded on the Software Media. These limitations may include a requirement that after using the program for a specified period of time, the user must pay a registration fee or discontinue use. By opening the Software packet(s), you will be agreeing to abide by the licenses and restrictions for these individual programs that are detailed in the About the CD-ROM appendix and on the Software Media. None of the material on this Software Media or listed in this Book may ever be redistributed, in original or modified form, for commercial purposes.

5. **Limited Warranty.**

   (a) WPI warrants that the Software and Software Media are free from defects in materials and workmanship under normal use for a period of sixty (60) days from the date of purchase of this Book. If WPI receives notification within the warranty period of defects in materials or workmanship, WPI will replace the defective Software Media.

   (b) WPI AND THE AUTHOR(S) OF THE BOOK DISCLAIM ALL OTHER WARRANTIES, EXPRESS OR IMPLIED, INCLUDING WITHOUT LIMITATION IMPLIED WARRANTIES OF MERCHANTABILITY AND FITNESS FOR A PARTICULAR PURPOSE, WITH RESPECT TO THE SOFTWARE, THE PROGRAMS, THE SOURCE CODE CONTAINED THEREIN, AND/OR THE TECHNIQUES DESCRIBED IN THIS BOOK. WPI DOES NOT WARRANT THAT THE FUNCTIONS CONTAINED IN THE SOFTWARE WILL MEET YOUR REQUIREMENTS OR THAT THE OPERATION OF THE SOFTWARE WILL BE ERROR FREE.

   (c) This limited warranty gives you specific legal rights, and you may have other rights that vary from jurisdiction to jurisdiction.

6. **Remedies.**

   (a) WPI's entire liability and your exclusive remedy for defects in materials and workmanship shall be limited to replacement of the Software Media, which may be returned to WPI with a copy of your receipt at the following address: Software Media Fulfillment Department, Attn.: *Signing For Dummies,* Wiley Publishing, Inc., 10475 Crosspoint Blvd., Indianapolis, IN 46256, or call 1-800-762-2974. Please allow four to six weeks for delivery. This Limited Warranty is void if failure of the Software Media has resulted from accident, abuse, or misapplication. Any replacement Software Media will be warranted for the remainder of the original warranty period or thirty (30) days, whichever is longer.

   (b) In no event shall WPI or the author be liable for any damages whatsoever (including without limitation damages for loss of business profits, business interruption, loss of business information, or any other pecuniary loss) arising from the use of or inability to use the Book or the Software, even if WPI has been advised of the possibility of such damages.

   (c) Because some jurisdictions do not allow the exclusion or limitation of liability for consequential or incidental damages, the above limitation or exclusion may not apply to you.

7. **U.S. Government Restricted Rights.** Use, duplication, or disclosure of the Software for or on behalf of the United States of America, its agencies and/or instrumentalities "U.S. Government" is subject to restrictions as stated in paragraph (c)(1)(ii) of the Rights in Technical Data and Computer Software clause of DFARS 252.227-7013, or subparagraphs (c) (1) and (2) of the Commercial Computer Software - Restricted Rights clause at FAR 52.227-19, and in similar clauses in the NASA FAR supplement, as applicable.

8. **General.** This Agreement constitutes the entire understanding of the parties and revokes and supersedes all prior agreements, oral or written, between them and may not be modified or amended except in a writing signed by both parties hereto that specifically refers to this Agreement. This Agreement shall take precedence over any other documents that may be in conflict herewith. If any one or more provisions contained in this Agreement are held by any court or tribunal to be invalid, illegal, or otherwise unenforceable, each and every other provision shall remain in full force and effect.

FOR DUMMIES®

A world of resources to help you grow

HOME, GARDEN & HOBBIES

Feng Shui
0-7645-5295-3

Gardening
0-7645-5130-2

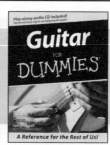

Guitar
0-7645-5106-X

Also available:

Auto Repair For Dummies
(0-7645-5089-6)

Chess For Dummies
(0-7645-5003-9)

Home Maintenance For Dummies
(0-7645-5215-5)

Organizing For Dummies
(0-7645-5300-3)

Piano For Dummies
(0-7645-5105-1)

Poker For Dummies
(0-7645-5232-5)

Quilting For Dummies
(0-7645-5118-3)

Rock Guitar For Dumm
(0-7645-5356-9)

Roses For Dummies
(0-7645-5202-3)

Sewing For Dummies
(0-7645-5137-X)

FOOD & WINE

Cooking
0-7645-5250-3

Cookies
0-7645-5390-9

Wine
0-7645-5114-0

Also available:

Bartending For Dummies
(0-7645-5051-9)

Chinese Cooking For Dummies
(0-7645-5247-3)

Christmas Cooking For Dummies
(0-7645-5407-7)

Diabetes Cookbook For Dummies
(0-7645-5230-9)

Grilling For Dummies
(0-7645-5076-4)

Low-Fat Cooking For Dummies
(0-7645-5035-7)

Slow Cookers For Dum
(0-7645-5240-6)

TRAVEL

Italy
0-7645-5453-0

Hawaii
0-7645-5438-7

Las Vegas
0-7645-5448-4

Also available:

America's National Parks For Dummies
(0-7645-6204-5)

Caribbean For Dummies
(0-7645-5445-X)

Cruise Vacations For Dummies 2003
(0-7645-5459-X)

Europe For Dummies
(0-7645-5456-5)

Ireland For Dummies
(0-7645-6199-5)

France For Dummies
(0-7645-6292-4)

London For Dummies
(0-7645-5416-6)

Mexico's Beach Resorts Dummies
(0-7645-6262-2)

Paris For Dummies
(0-7645-5494-8)

RV Vacations For Dumm
(0-7645-5443-3)

Walt Disney World & Or For Dummies
(0-7645-5444-1)

Available wherever books are sold. Go to www.dummies.com or call 1-877-762-2974 to order direct.

FOR DUMMIES®

Plain-English solutions for everyday challenges

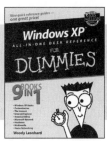
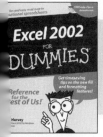
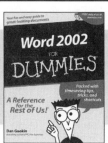

FOR DUMMIES®

Helping you expand your horizons and realize your potential

INTERNET

0-7645-0894-6

0-7645-1659-0

0-7645-1642-6

Also available:

America Online 7.0 For Dummies
(0-7645-1624-8)

Genealogy Online For Dummies
(0-7645-0807-5)

The Internet All-in-One Desk Reference For Dummies
(0-7645-1659-0)

Internet Explorer 6 For Dummies
(0-7645-1344-3)

The Internet For Dummies Quick Reference
(0-7645-1645-0)

Internet Privacy For Dumm
(0-7645-0846-6)

Researching Online For Dummies
(0-7645-0546-7)

Starting an Online Busines For Dummies
(0-7645-1655-8)

DIGITAL MEDIA

0-7645-1664-7

0-7645-1675-2

0-7645-0806-7

Also available:

CD and DVD Recording For Dummies
(0-7645-1627-2)

Digital Photography All-in-One Desk Reference For Dummies
(0-7645-1800-3)

Digital Photography For Dummies Quick Reference
(0-7645-0750-8)

Home Recording for Musicians For Dummies
(0-7645-1634-5)

MP3 For Dummies
(0-7645-0858-X)

Paint Shop Pro "X" For Dummies
(0-7645-2440-2)

Photo Retouching & Restoration For Dummies
(0-7645-1662-0)

Scanners For Dummies
(0-7645-0783-4)

GRAPHICS

0-7645-0817-2

0-7645-1651-5

0-7645-0895-4

Also available:

Adobe Acrobat 5 PDF For Dummies
(0-7645-1652-3)

Fireworks 4 For Dummies
(0-7645-0804-0)

Illustrator 10 For Dummies
(0-7645-3636-2)

QuarkXPress 5 For Dumr
(0-7645-0643-9)

Visio 2000 For Dummies
(0-7645-0635-8)

Available wherever books are sold. Go to www.dummies.com or call 1-877-762-2974 to order direct.

FOR DUMMIES®

The advice and explanations you need to succeed

[SE]LF-HELP, SPIRITUALITY & RELIGION

Sex
0-7645-5302-X

Parenting
0-7645-5418-2

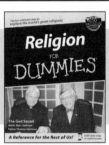

Religion
0-7645-5264-3

Also available:

The Bible For Dummies
(0-7645-5296-1)

Buddhism For Dummies
(0-7645-5359-3)

Christian Prayer For Dummies
(0-7645-5500-6)

Dating For Dummies
(0-7645-5072-1)

Judaism For Dummies
(0-7645-5299-6)

Potty Training For Dummies
(0-7645-5417-4)

Pregnancy For Dummies
(0-7645-5074-8)

Rekindling Romance For Dummies
(0-7645-5303-8)

Spirituality For Dummies
(0-7645-5298-8)

Weddings For Dummies
(0-7645-5055-1)

[PET]S

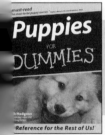

Puppies
0-7645-5255-4

Dog Training
0-7645-5286-4

Cats
0-7645-5275-9

Also available:

Labrador Retrievers For Dummies
(0-7645-5281-3)

Aquariums For Dummies
(0-7645-5156-6)

Birds For Dummies
(0-7645-5139-6)

Dogs For Dummies
(0-7645-5274-0)

Ferrets For Dummies
(0-7645-5259-7)

German Shepherds For Dummies
(0-7645-5280-5)

Golden Retrievers For Dummies
(0-7645-5267-8)

Horses For Dummies
(0-7645-5138-8)

Jack Russell Terriers For Dummies
(0-7645-5268-6)

Puppies Raising & Training Diary For Dummies
(0-7645-0876-8)

[EDU]CATION & TEST PREPARATION

Spanish
0-7645-5194-9

Algebra
0-7645-5325-9

The ACT
0-7645-5210-4

Also available:

Chemistry For Dummies
(0-7645-5430-1)

English Grammar For Dummies
(0-7645-5322-4)

French For Dummies
(0-7645-5193-0)

The GMAT For Dummies
(0-7645-5251-1)

Inglés Para Dummies
(0-7645-5427-1)

Italian For Dummies
(0-7645-5196-5)

Research Papers For Dummies
(0-7645-5426-3)

The SAT I For Dummies
(0-7645-5472-7)

U.S. History For Dummies
(0-7645-5249-X)

World History For Dummies
(0-7645-5242-2)

Available wherever books are sold. Go to www.dummies.com or call 1-877-762-2974 to order direct.

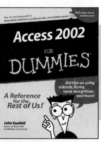